FINLAND

Helsinki

WEDEN

Stockholm

openhagen

Moscow

Warsaw

U S S R

POLAND

rague

CZECHOSLOVAKIA

nna

Budapest

HUNGARY

RUMANIA

Bucharest

Belgrade

YUGOSLAVIA

BULGARIA

Sofia

ALBANIA

Tiranë

Ankara

GREECE

TURKEY

Athens

Nicosia

CYPRUS

TREKKING IN
EUROPE

AA

TREKKING IN
EUROPE

Texts by
Giancarlo Corbellini

AA

Translated by John Gilbert

Photographs by:

Agenzia Stradella
Archivio Folco Quilici
Massimo Capuani
Giancarlo Corbellini
Massimo Dalla Chiesa
Mario De Biasi
Alessandra De Faveri
Alfredo Favre
Fulvio Favre
Franco Figari
Focus Team
Albano Marcarini
A. Martin
Renato Onofri
Fabio Penati
Daniela Pulvirenti
Italo Zandonella

Distributed in the United Kingdom by the Publishing Division of The Automobile Association,
Fanum House, Basingstoke, Hampshire RG21 2EA.

This edition published 1990 by The Automobile Association,
Fanum House, Basingstoke, Hampshire RG21 2EA.

A CIP catalogue record for this book is available from the British
Library.

ISBN 0 7495 0187 1

Typeset by Rowland Phototypesetting Ltd, Bury St Edmunds, Suffolk.
Printed and bound in Italy by Arnoldo Mondadori Editore, Verona

CONTENTS

INTRODUCTION

An early nineteenth-century English traveller who made a long journey over the Alps of northern Italy into Switzerland declared that in the space of three weeks he had never walked along any road wide enough to take a two-wheeled cart.

In the Europe of today such a situation would be unthinkable. Cradle of the Industrial Revolution, all European nations have seen a massive increase in population which has slowly but surely given rise to the transformation of primitive natural surroundings into agricultural, industrial and urban areas. Few places are inaccessible to man: side roads lead to the most isolated valleys, while cablecars and chairlifts carry tourists up to the level of glaciers and mountain tops. In fact, trekking, in the true sense of walking age-old routes made up for the most part of bridle paths, footpaths and sheep tracks, becomes more difficult every year.

Despite this extensive distribution of mankind, Europe, even today, has areas of truly wild, untouched country, often protected within parks or natural reserves, where it is still possible to live the experience of authentic walking, hiking and trekking, putting up with fatigue and discomfort in a quest for uncontaminated surroundings, natural beauty and moving experiences.

First, there are the great mountain ranges which offer infinite itineraries over ancient systems of roads and crossways formed over time to link villages and summer pastures. By following these pastoral trails, it is possible to plan long treks in stages, with convenient stops in villages or mountain huts.

Secondly, there are vast stretches of northern Europe covered with dense conifer woods, and, still farther north, with the sparse growth of birch and ground vegetation which characterizes the tundra. This is the ideal environment for anyone who takes pleasure in unblemished nature and wishes to explore it under their own steam, armed only with a rucksack packed with the essentials for camping.

This guide, however, also suggests trekking itineraries in other areas which are less likely to come to mind and cover a wider range of surroundings that might be expected. In the case of each of these environments we have chosen the most impressive itineraries, with emphasis on those which are still situated as far away as possible from roads and which follow paths, trails and forest tracks through areas of considerable natural beauty.

As well as the sheer enjoyment of healthy physical activity, these treks also provide the opportunity to make contact with a world constantly under threat; a small world, perhaps, but one that still retains genuine values and authentic traditions that industrialization and technological progress have not completely wiped out, and which needs to be understood, protected and preserved.

All the trips described in this guide are ideal for those who like to travel independently and at their own pace. For them Europe still has some wonderful surprises in store.

Degrees of difficulty

Each itinerary as a whole, and its intermediate stages, is given a letter symbol which indicates its comparative degree of difficulty. For present purposes four different levels of suitability are listed: R (Rambler), H (Hiker), E (Expert Hiker) and EE (Expert hiker with Equipment).

Each set of initials thus conveys an overall assessment of the itinerary concerned and takes into account the following factors:

– type of route (lane, path, trail or track, etc.), terrain (wood, grassland, stony ground, etc.) and surface (broken, smooth, uneven, etc.).

– presence of signposting (direction posts, painted signs, piles of stones, etc.).

– change in elevation.

– steepness of route.

– possible difficulties of orientation or traceability.

– maximum height reached or altitude at which route takes place.

– steepness and exposure of slopes.

– technical difficulties (snow, rocks, etc.).

– type of equipment for rocky stretches (ladders, ropes).

– possible risks and dangers.

– duration.

– presence of camps, huts or stopover points.

– possible fords.

More specifically, the letters may be defined as follows:

R = Rambler. These itineraries follow easy paths, lanes and bridleways: they are clearly marked and thus pose no uncertainties, difficulties or problems of orientation. They occur at under 1,500 m (5,000 ft), with a maximum change in elevation of 500/600 m (1,650/2,000 ft). The time required for walking from one stopover point to another is not more than 2/3 hours. A minimum amount of physical preparation is needed. Overnight stays are always in accommodation with facilities (hotels, cabins, huts).

Itineraries listed as R: Kevo Canyon, Deer Trail, Bernina Trail, Mount Athos Tour.

H = Hiker. The itineraries follow longer paths and trails, with either smooth or broken surfaces, sometimes very narrow, or on rough tracks (meadows, rubble, stony ground); they may include some short, level or slightly sloping stretches of residual snow, but these will not present any danger even if you were to slip or fall. Parts of the route may be across open ground lacking paths, but they are always adequately signposted and pose no problems; they will require only some sense of orientation, slight familiarity with mountain terrain, training for walks, and appropriate footwear and equipment. Maps, a compass and a plan of the route will be useful.

In the case of long excursions, a backpack will be needed and overnight stays may be on camping sites or in bivouacs, mountain or wilderness huts. Where no bridges exist, all water courses are easy to cross.

Itineraries listed as H: Kevo Canyon, Bear Trail, Pembrokeshire Coast Path, Tour du Mont Blanc, Giants' Trail, Bernina Trail, Dolomites High-Level Walk No. 1, Corsican High-Level Route, Durmitor Park.

E = Expert Hiker. These are generally signposted itineraries but entail the capacity to cope with different and special types of terrain such as:

– trails over difficult or hazardous ground (steep slopes of rock or slippery grass, mixed rocks and grass, or rocks and scree);

– varying types of terrain at high altitude (stony ground, short, fairly level snowfields, open slopes without stopover points); maps and a compass are recommended;

– stretches of rocky terrain with slight technical difficulties, but fitted with climbing aids and signposted;

– short tracts of unfissured ice which can be crossed without the use of ropes, or any particular safety measures;

– fords over streams with uneven beds and strong currents.

These itineraries require: general mountain experience and familiarity with a mountain environment; a sure step; no fear of heights; adequate physical preparation; and appropriate equipment.

Itineraries listed as E: Bernina Trail, Corsican High-Level Route, Durmitor Park.

EE = Expert hiker with Equipment. These include the technically advanced climbing routes typical of the Dolomites which will have short stretches equipped with climbing aids, such as fixed iron cables, pegs or iron ladders, in exposed places. They are for the fit hiker with some skill in climbing and training in the use of safety equipment (carabiners, a basic harness and climbing rope).

Itineraries listed as EE: the Castelletto and Schiara stretches in the Dolomites High-Level Walk no. 1.

Note: the degree of difficulty refers to the period recommended for the particular trek. At other times of year the presence of snow and ice may increase potential difficulties.

How to use the guide

TIMES: the times for covering an itinerary are calculated on the average walking pace of a fit walker and do not take into account stops on the way. Bear in mind that they do not apply to single walks but to itineraries which are broken up into several (from three to ten) stages, so that many require training in long-distance hiking. Total and intermediate stage times are both given, however.

CHANGES IN ELEVATION: these are generally worked out by taking into account the difference between the minimum and maximum heights, be it gains or losses in elevation. When an itinerary involves many ascents and descents, the change in elevation given represents the sum total of the successive gains and losses. Changes in elevation are given for all mountain routes which have significant ascents and descents. They are therefore vital for appreciating the difficulties posed by a particular itinerary or stage, and assessing the level of training required.

DISTANCE: this is given for a long route over ground which is fairly flat and without significant changes in altitude. It is estimated by means of a map measurer or over the ground with a pedometer.

WALKING DIRECTION: the terms left and right are used with reference to the direction of walking.

ALTIMETRY: that given on the official maps of the countries where the itinerary is located.

SIGNPOSTING: when present, the type of sign is described as well as any applicable path or trail numbers.

EQUIPMENT: the necessary equipment for the various itineraries is abbreviated as follows: L (Low altitude); M (Mid-mountain); H (High altitude); B (Backpacking).

Low altitude (L) applies to routes running along coasts, across plains or among hills, on lanes or easy paths, or in mountain regions generally below 1,000 m (3,300 ft). Light trekking shoes with non-slip soles, sweater, shorts and cotton headwear are sufficient. Contents of your rucksack should include a tracksuit, a light windcheater and a water container.

L itineraries: Deer Trail, Pembrokeshire Coast Path, Mount Athos Tour.

Mid-mountain (M) itineraries are between 1,000 and 2,000 m (3,300–6,500 ft). The paths may include stretches of scree and steep grass slopes which will be slippery when wet. Essential equipment includes strong boots, long trousers, a heavy, waterproof windcheater (ideally gore-tex), a woollen sweater and a water container.

M itineraries: Durmitor Park.

High altitude (H): these routes lie above 2,000 m (6,500 ft), on rugged and broken ground in zones subject to sudden weather changes. At the highest altitudes there is a chance of snow even in midsummer. Obligatory equipment comprises strong boots, preferably waterproof for crossing snowy tracts (gaiters are also useful for keeping bottoms of trousers dry and snow out of boots), loose hiking trousers or salopettes, a sweater, a jacket (preferably gore-tex), gloves and a woollen cap, sunglasses, water container, map and a compass.

H itineraries: Tour du Mont Blanc, Giants' Trail, Bernina Trail, Dolomite High-Level Walk, Corsican High-Level Route.

Backpacking (B): long hikes with backpacks loaded with provisions for overnight stays in tents, cabins or unlocked wilderness huts. Necessary equipment therefore includes cooking apparatus (camping stove, pots, cutlery, etc.), essential foodstuffs, tent, camping mat and sleeping bag. For a week-long trek you will probably need a rucksack that will carry about 15 kg (33 lb) plus any photographic equipment you wish to take.

B itineraries: all those in Scandinavia.

MAPS: those indicated are the official maps of the countries concerned, although often these are not up to date and not designed particularly for rambling and trekking. In such cases it is best to buy maps compiled by small publishing houses. There is usually a wide range varying in scale and detail to be found locally.

PROTECTION OF THE ENVIRONMENT: some itineraries run through parks or nature reserves and require you to adhere to the specified regulations of the place. Others cross non-protected areas, but here too it is essential to care for the environment. Of all tourist activities, trekking causes the least pollution, but it still needs common sense and consideration, and the observance of the basic rule never to light fires, except in the sites provided, or leave behind any trace of one's presence. It is a good idea to carry a bag in your rucksack to put any rubbish in. At the end of the day's walk this can then be deposited in a suitable container. All visitors to these areas of natural beauty should remember that by marring their immediate surroundings in any way they will precipitate the degradation of the few places left where man is truly at one with nature.

The European Long-Distance Footpaths

Alongside certain itineraries, next to the specific signposting, you may find a red and white shield marked E1, E2, E3, etc. These are the routes of the European Long-Distance Footpaths prepared by the European Ramblers' Association to which 36 national associations are affiliated.

The E.R.A. is responsible for the upkeep of eight such trails which link the main points of the continent from north to south and east to west. These are as follows:

– North Sea to Mediterranean Sea. E1: North Sea (Flensburg) – Lake Constance – Gotthard – Mediterranean Sea (Genoa Pegli), 2,800 km (1,740 miles). E2: North Sea (Ostend) – Lake Geneva – Mediterranean Sea (Nice), 2,600 km (1,615 miles). For E1, work is proceeding on the extension along the entire range of the Apennines to Syracuse.

– Atlantic Ocean to Bohemian Forest. E3: Atlantic (Roncevaux) – Ardennes – Bohemian Forest (Marktredwitz), 2,600 km (1,615 miles).

– Pyrenees to Lake Balaton. E4: Montserrat – Jura – Constance – Salzburg – Vienna – Budapest, 3,500 km (2,175 miles).

– Lake Constance to Adriatic Sea. E5: Constance – Bregenz – Sonthofen – Bolzano – Verona, 600 km (372 miles).

– Baltic Sea to Adriatic Sea. E6: Copenhagen – Lübeck – Coburg – Marktredwitz – Nobelstein – Mariazell – Rijeka, 2,800 km (1,740 miles).

– Atlantic Ocean to Slovenia. E7: Lisbon – Madrid – Lourdes – Carcassonne – Nice – Genoa – Lake Garda – Skofje Loka – Kumrovec, 4,200 km (2,604 miles): under construction.

– North Sea to Carpathians. E8: Amsterdam – Aachen – Bonn – Koblenz – Passau – Vienna – Hainburg, 2,200 km (1,365 miles).

They are, naturally, very long itineraries which take in the most diverse types of environment from plains and hills to high mountains. Where necessary, they follow normal roads. There are, therefore, stretches of great interest to ramblers alternating with others which form part of the journey merely for convenience's sake.

The map of the European Long-Distance Footpaths with their brief summary can be obtained from the E.R.A., EWV-Geschäftsstelle Reichsstrasse 4, D-6600, Saarbrücken, Federal German Republic.

The great mountain ranges

The mountain regions of Europe, criss-crossed with innumerable paths and tracks, provide one of the most rewarding and popular settings for serious trekking.

Apart from the valley floors and those zones which, because of their favourable layout, have been developed as summer and winter tourist resorts, the mountains represent the most extensive areas of pure wilderness in central and southern Europe.

Theirs is a world of rocks and ice, meadows and lakes, which can sometimes be reached only by way of steep and tiresome tracks. Here, the lonely sound of tinkling cowbells is a reassuring testimony to the fact that the mountain people are determined to preserve their age-old habits and traditions come what may.

In these surroundings the last truly wild animals of Europe still roam in their natural habitat and precious examples of alpine flowers are protected in national parks and reserves.

Walking the slopes and foothills of these mountains or trekking from valley to valley and from hut to hut is to come very close to nature and one's roots, and to benefit from a rich gamut of new and varied experiences.

The terrain here is never easy and as a rule treks involve a succession of climbs and descents. So hikers should possess at least a modicum of mountain experience, and be suitably fit and equipped.

Because of the altitude, it is best to do the listed treks in July or August since until late spring and by late autumn it is possible to encounter unfavourable snowy conditions.

The European continent

The dense forest exerts an indefinable attraction often mingled with feelings of unease and fear – sensations reinforced by childhood fairy tales such as "Hansel and Gretel" and "Little Red Riding Hood" or legends like that of the Nibelungs. It is not by chance that such stories originated in this dark and eerie environment.

Exploitation of the land for agriculture in the Middle Ages and the urban development of the Industrial Revolution have nevertheless led to the steady but thorough destruction of the vast stretches of uninterrupted woodland which once covered the continent.

This has rendered it all the more important, however, to preserve the last remnants of forest which appear as islands of greenery amid the huge areas of farmland and urban sprawl. A network of country paths and trails links small villages and isolated farming communities, which still look to the woods and pastures for their livelihood. Walking these paths at leisure in the shade of conifers and broadleaved trees, with their subtle changes of seasonal colour, helps to foster an appreciation for enduring traditions and an understanding of the true relationship between man and his origins.

The Black Forest in Germany, setting for the Deer Trail, is perhaps the most representative example of this continental landscape. The depths of the forest mantle the slopes of gently rounded mountains, modest in height, and criss-crossed by countless paths which make for easy walks. These include convenient round trips that are especially suitable for family groups and older people. Late spring and autumn are ideal seasons for walking here.

Around the Mediterranean

The Mediterranean conjures up images of golden beaches and holiday crowds, and of course millions of tourists from central and northern Europe do descend on its shores every year to enjoy the sunshine and the warm sea. Probably no other region in Europe has been so radically transformed by the activities stemming from this tide of tourism.

In fact, the characteristic Mediterranean vegetation, the maquis, survives only in restricted zones that have been geographically isolated and nowadays most often protected in parks and nature reserves. The hinterland, away from the coasts, on the other hand, often tends to be neglected and for that very reason still has a rich tradition of material and spiritual culture. Trekking, as a far less instrusive form of tourism, constitutes the best way of rediscovering and helping to maintain this local culture.

Two Mediterranean itineraries are suggested. One runs through the wild and solitary mountain regions of the Corsican interior. The second links the principal monasteries of Mount Athos on the Halkidiki peninsula of Greece (women not permitted entry). This is a corner of coastline which, for historical reasons, has remained intact and which can be discovered only on foot along cobbled tracks which are in parts carpeted with the luscious Mediterranean maquis and which elsewhere skirt cliffs hanging sheer above the sea.

The trek across Corsica should be done between late spring and early autumn; the visit to Mount Athos can be made at almost any time of year, bearing in mind any access restrictions in force.

The seas of the north

Precipitous cliffs, rock arches eroded by the force of storms, a coastline battered by winds, stripped bare of trees but blooming with colourful wild flowers, endless beaches of fine sand or smooth pebbles often exposed to violent high tides – all these are among the most spectacular and exciting features of the ocean environment. The influence of the sea can also be felt inland where fields, moors, marshes and hills are often swathed in mist; and these are the elements of a typical ramble through farmlands and villages, from areas of human presence to places untouched by civilization.

In the rolling countryside, continually eroded on its coastline, the ancient system of enclosed fields still prevails, creating a mosaic pattern of pastures and arable land where the unnatural silence is broken only by the distant squealing of gulls and the swishing roar of waves breaking against the rocks.

This environment is typical of the Pembrokeshire National Park in South Wales, where a long and easily negotiable coastal path offers a wonderful opportunity for walking. The best time for doing this trip is normally spring to early summer.

The Far North

Nowadays the roads of Scandinavian Lapland (conventionally understood to be the territory north of the Arctic Circle) are busy with cars, caravans and trailers heading for North Cape; and you can stop at the stalls set up by the Lapps along the Arctic Road to buy souvenirs or to take pictures of the reindeer. Nevertheless Lapland is much more than a ribbon of asphalt snaking through the vast Arctic landscape towards a tourist spot that risks becoming too commercialized.

The only way to appreciate the land's hidden wonders is to explore it on foot. This is to enter a natural world far more varied and interesting than might at first glance be imagined and to experience those powerful sensations which can only come from travelling through a total wilderness.

The typical landscape is that of the taiga, with enormous forests of conifers which thin out gradually as you go further north, and of the tundra, a barren and empty wasteland stretching to distant horizons.

This is the classic terrain for backpacking, which demands complete self-sufficiency because of the absence of all facilities. The itineraries are relatively easy but this is offset by the need to carry all your equipment in your rucksack.

Treks are best done in the summer months which offer the best climatic conditions.

FINLAND

KEVO CANYON

The tundra

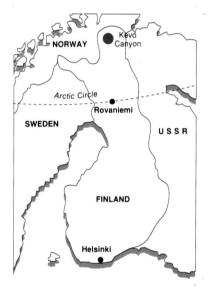

Useful addresses: Finnish National Board of Forestry – P.O. box 233-00121 Helsinki, 1-tel: (9)0/6163 or Inari district office tel: (9)697/21951.
Map: Map of Kevo – scale 1:100,000 available in Helsinki, from the following addresses: Akateeminen Kirjakauppa-Keskuskatu, 1-00101 Helsinki; Karttakeskus Espa-Etlaesplanadi, 10-00130 Helsinki.
Bibliography: Some information accompanies the recommended map.

In northern Lapland, between latitudes 69° and 70°N, the wild landscape of the tundra, with its boundless stretches of largely unpopulated territory, is suddenly interrupted by the deep gorge of the Kevo River, formed millions of years ago and subsequently reshaped by the action of glaciers during the last Ice Age. This deep cleft in the undulating Lapp landscape can be followed on foot, partly along the edge of the plateau and partly by descending the marked path to the banks of the Kevo beneath.

The trail, which runs for 64 km (40 miles), provides an opportunity to discover a region which is unique for the relative mildness of its climate: although it lies more than 300 km (185 miles) above the Arctic Circle, plants flourish here with a profusion that seems unthinkable in such latitudes.

For this reason, Kevo Canyon became an area protected for its great natural and scientific interest, and since 1956 it has been a nature reserve, extended westwards in 1982 to include the Paistuoddar Fells with the highest peak of Kuivi (641 m/2,102 ft).

Flora and fauna

On the undulating slopes of the high plateau, which were far more in relief before the pressure of ice remodelled them, mosses and lichens are the life forms that survive the harsh Arctic climate. In the sheltered spots, however, the vegetation is more varied, ranging from tangled, creeping shrubs (dwarf

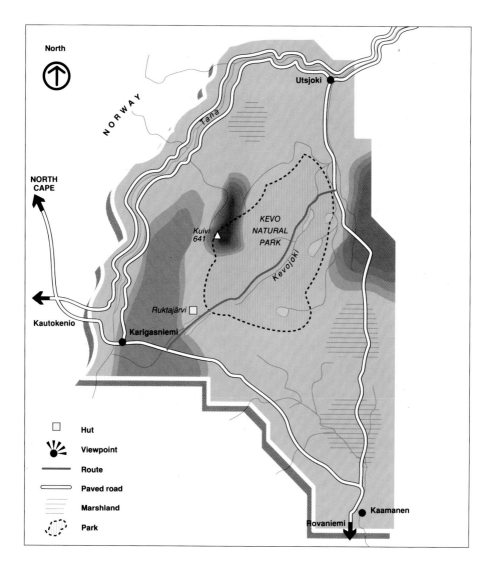

Distance: 64 km (40 miles), divided into four stages.

Departure point: The path leaves from state highway 4 (main road for North Cape), about 420 km (260 miles) north of Rovaniemi, capital of Finnish Lapland, and 10 km (6¼ miles) east of Karigasniemi, a small town on the border of Finland and Norway. There is space for parking and a board indicating route through park.

Arrival point: The itinerary ends at the state highway between Utsjoki (on the border of Finland and Norway) and Kaamanen (Inari) near the Kenesjarvi campsite. Subsequent return to the car made easier by checking times of local bus services prior to departure.

Where to stay: The only unlocked fell hut (unattended but with radiotelephone) is that of Ruktajärvi, on the southern edge of the reserve. On the rest of the route there are sites fitted out for pitching tents, with place for fire, wood pile and toilet, and equipped with radiotelephone (third stage).

Signposting: Red marking on tree bark and rocks; in the reserve you are not allowed to leave the marked paths.

Difficulty: H – Hiker; R – Rambler.

Best period: July–August.

Equipment: Mid-mountain; suitable clothing for protection against rain, sudden changes of temperature and mosquitoes; mosquito repellents; sufficient food, equipment, and provisions for the entire journey.

heathers) to woods of downy birch (*Betula pubescens* var. *tortuosa*), with fantastically twisted trunks, in the better protected valleys. Here, concealed from the attacks of lurking birds of prey, various species of tundra birds make their nests.

To the east, in a zone of moors and peatland, there are several large lakes surrounded by innumerable tiny, interlinking pools which each constitute a miniature habitat of their own. These are the destinations for migrating species, providing homes and nesting sites for the rich variety of Lapland's birdlife. Due to the basic necessity of finding food, the presence of large predators (golden eagle, buzzard, peregrine falcon and snowy owl) is in direct proportion to the number of small mammals (hares and rabbits) and, above all, to the abundance of rodents, notably voles and that fascinating creature whose life is of constant fascination to man, the lemming.

It is while you are descending and the scenery around you is changing completely that the deep-cut valley makes its greatest impression. The Kevo carves out its course at the bottom where, because of the particularly favourable climate, the conifer forest reappears, far beyond the limits of the taiga. While from the plateau above come the echoes of the reindeer bellowing in the distance, inside the valley itself the harsh terrain offers refuge to several animals of shy temperament, in particular the rare Arctic fox.

Situated in the northern part of the reserve is the Kevo Subarctic Research Institute of the University of Turku, engaged in the scientific investigation of the ecology of the subarctic regions.

The itinerary

Entry to the reserve is restricted to the routes marked on the map. For additional information and special requests, apply to the district office of the National Forest Authority at Inari (tel. (9)697-21951). Keep strictly to the path, always clearly marked in red. For this trek it is essential to have a tent to sleep in and a supply of food and provisions for 3/4 days. (See box *Useful Advice*).

USEFUL ADVICE

When to go: July and August are the best months as regards the weather, although mosquitoes are at their worst in July. September is a good month because there are beautiful autumn colours and fewer mosquitoes, which vanish completely with the first frosts. However, it does of course get colder and the weather is more variable.

Clothing: The standard list of clothing for treks of several days in Lapland must include waterproof items, ideally in gore-tex. Bear in mind also the possible need to keep the rucksack itself sheltered from the rain. Gaiters may be useful in damp areas and, following the Finnish example, Wellington boots to ford streams; otherwise the simplest method is to take off your boots every time and tackle the cold water barefoot.

A long-sleeved shirt and long trousers are essential to protect all parts of the body from mosquito bites.

Equipment: Among articles which must not be forgotten are a compass, a good map, insect repellent, tent, sleeping bag, camping mat, camping stove, fuel and food, preferably the specially freeze-dried, lightweight brands.

On pages 16 and 17: on the plateau, at the edges of the Kevo Canyon, is a graveyard of willow and birch destroyed by a natural epidemic.

THE LAPP MINORITY

The ancient population of Lapps (Sámi), which has lived in Scandinavia for several thousand years, is now reduced to just over 50,000 individuals, of whom 5,000 live in Finland. Formerly hunters and fishermen, the Lapps have learned over the centuries how to raise reindeer (rock carvings from Alta in Norway, which go back 6,000 years, offer an example of Arctic life among the earliest inhabitants), but today they are also engaged in agriculture, the manufacture of articles in wood and reindeer skin for the tourist trade, and various other skills. For a section of the Lapp population in Sweden, the raising of reindeer is still their main source of income; however, in order to make it a profitable activity, each family must own at least 500 animals.

The ancient form of nomadism which compelled entire families to move about, following the migrations of the reindeer from the conifer taiga to the high plateau, is now confined to the times when the animals are herded together for branding and slaughtering. With modern means of communication and new access roads, it is no longer necessary to live all year round with the deer. Motorcycles, motor sledges and sometimes even aeroplanes are used to round up the reindeer which at other times graze wild on the tundra.

From state highway 4 to the Ruktajärvi fell hut   R

11.5 km (7 miles), 3 hours

To reach the only hut situated on the southern edge of the reserve, you can leave (from state highway 4, some 10 km/6 miles east of Karigasniemi) as late as early afternoon. At these latitudes, in fact, there is no likelihood of being overtaken by darkness and this first stage, which is regarded as a transit stage, can be treated as a simple warm-up for the more demanding routes encountered in the days to come.

The first stretch of the walk is a succession of ups and downs over gently undulating ground, morainic in origin, covered with dense tree growth not more than 3–4 m (10–13 ft) high: this is willow and birch woodland, the typical landscape of the *ruska*, which presents an extraordinary display of autumn colours all of a sudden when the season changes.

The track winds its way across sandy terrain among pools and lake basins of ancient glacial origin, and on its descent to the banks of Lake Stuorra it becomes a dirt path. It skirts the lake for its entire length and leads to the Ruktajärvi camp across a marshy area over a wooden track, conveniently laid over the wet ground by the Scandinavian authorities without defacing the environment in any way.

The camp and unlocked hut (sleeps 10 on wooden beds) is on a large area of flat, open, sandy ground ringed by a square of tree trunks, with a place for a fire, a store of wood and a cabin that serves as a toilet. The surrounding vegetation, though formed of many different species, is strangely reminiscent of the bush of the African savannas.

Ruktajärvi to the first camping site   H

18.5 km (11½ miles), about 6 hours

The path, continuing just after Ruktajärvi, leads into the Natural Park. The scenery is similar to that of the previous day. The occasional small woodland clearings were once ponds that have now dried out. Reindeer sometimes wander up to graze on the soft carpet of grass and moss growing from the gravel. Then the geological configuration of the terrain changes appearance. The track follows the ridges of a depression which extends far towards the horizon, giving advance notice of the spectacular Kevo Canyon.

THE TUNDRA MOSSES AND LICHENS

While walking through the boundless and often desolate landscape of northern Lapland, it is worth taking the time to observe the vegetation of the tundra. The initial impression is that it is rather sparse but, by paying attention to what passes underfoot, you will notice a wealth of different plants.

The word tundra is derived from the Finnish word *tunturi*, meaning a mound or hill. It describes a special type of terrain which is slightly undulating and devoid of tree growth, as is found in the Finno–Sarmatian shield carved out by repeated extensions of the ice during the Pleistocene.

Beyond the Arctic Circle the harsh climate, despite the warming flow of the Gulf Stream along the Norwegian coasts, allows only the surface of the soil to thaw out during the brief summer, while the rest remains permanently frozen. This is the phenomenon of permafrost which prevents roots developing in the ground.

Here is the kingdom of the mosses and lichens. In marshy zones there are many varieties of moss in contrasting colours, and among them grows the *lakka*, the choice Arctic cloudberry, rich orange-yellow with a bitter taste, from which the liquor of that name is prepared. Gathering it is a profitable activity and an important economic resource for the local people. The tundra of lichen, on the other hand, is characteristic of drier ground with soft layers of peat. It is interesting to identify the commoner species such as *Parmelia sulcata*, *Xanthoria parientina* (reputed in the Middle Ages to be an infallible medicine against jaundice) and *Cladonia rangiferina*, known as reindeer lichen. Each lichen forms a microscopic forest at ground level and one component of the tundra's huge mosaic. It is, in fact, no ordinary plant, for it comprises two co-existent vegetable organisms, a fungus and an alga which, thanks to symbiosis, manage to withstand the rigours of the Arctic climate.

Lichens grow a few millimeters a year but are extraordinarily tenacious and long lived. Capable of resisting snow, wind and frost, they are nevertheless vulnerable to atmospheric pollution. Their property of absorbing radioactive substances and storing them for a long time became evident after the Chernobyl nuclear explosion which polluted the Lapp tundra to the point of forcing the Swedish authorities to slaughter thousands of reindeer which had eaten lichens.

Branding the reindeer: skilfully wielding the lassoo, this Lapp looks for the ownership mark on the mother reindeer before catching the baby following her.

About four hours have passed since leaving the camp: the open and partially stony tundra now gives way to birch woods and shortly after you reach a site prepared for camping. A little farther on the Kevo River suddenly comes into sight, rushing in a powerful torrent, creating successive layers of different ecosystems which are each of great scientific interest.

The path continues along the left bank of the Kevo on the edge of the valley and then veers away once more to the plateau. After about two hours' walking across the undulating tundra, the roar of a waterfall signals the descent to the first equipped camping site in the valley proper. The waterfall of Fiellokeadgge-jokka, a tributary of the Kevo, has a drop of 30 m (100 ft) carved out by the glaciers that formed the main valley in a typical U-shape. Steps have been built down the winding path which leads over the ford and to the site where tents can be pitched overnight.

Inside the canyon, from camping site to camping site   H

23 km (14¼ miles), 7/8 hours

This is the most interesting and attractive stage, which involves climbing twice up to the plateau and back down into the canyon. And it is on top, as you walk through a whole forest of willows and birches destroyed years ago by a natural epidemic, that you realize how delicate the ecological balance really is in Lapland. Swarms of insects devoured the leaves of the trees before they had time to carry out photosynthesis, so preventing the storage of vital energy to withstand the winter. The subsequent invasion of lemmings eliminated this insect plague, but too late.

In the first stretch of plateau (10 km/6¼ miles) there are distant views to the north-west to the snow-capped peaks of the Kuivi and Paistunturi ranges, and to the north-east to the huge lake basin of Vuogojärvi. The dismal landscape of dead forest, like a cemetery of white, twisted trunks, also covers the entire second part of the plateau walk (8 km/5 miles). Here, among the dried skeletons of wood,

THE ARCTIC NIGHT

In summer, Lapland is bathed in sunlight, day and night. For anyone from further south, the phenomenon of a non-existent summer night is the most striking and fascinating feature of this Arctic land. When you can come across other walkers along the paths at virtually any time in a span of 24 hours, you begin to understand the true way of life of those who live here right through the year: a strong urge for life and for light before the arrival of the *kaamos*, the long Arctic night. For every living thing, humans included, summer is lived to the full in preparation for winter. So even at midnight you may come across someone varnishing the sauna or repairing the farmhouse roof. The same instinct for survival also urges plants and animals, engaged continuously in reproduction, to take advantage of this phenomenon, even though the sun's rays, filtering through the atmosphere at an exceptionally oblique angle, lose their energy and provide no warmth during the Arctic night.

At Utsjoki (69°52′N), in the extreme northern sector of Finnish Lapland, near the Kevo Natural Park, the sun is visible at midnight between 16 May and 28 July; in winter, on the other hand, the long polar night lasts from 24 November to 17 January. But there is never complete darkness: the aurora borealis, the reflection of snow and sunlight which casts a hidden glow from under the horizon, prevents it from being pitch dark.

LEMMENJOKI NATIONAL PARK

Features: This is the largest park in Finland, 2,800 km² (1,081 sq. miles) in area, which together with the adjoining Norwegian park of Ovre Anarjokka, represents one of the most extensive protected areas in Europe. Lying between the Norwegian frontier and state highway 955, the park, opened in 1956, covers a huge uninhabited area: to the south-west it consists of a level plain covered with rivers and bogs; to the north-east the terrain is more hilly.

Ancient enclosures for branding reindeer show that these places were, and to some extent still are, important to the Lapps as pasture ground for their herds. Another interesting feature is the presence, in certain streams, of gold which, after the intense activities of earlier times, is now only extracted by a few nostalgic prospectors.

Access and information centers: All information and access can be found in the village of Njurgalahti, accessible from Inari by a secondary road branching off state highway 955. From Inari there are air-taxi helicopter services on request. Lemmenkoji National Park: Office of park superintendent – Njurgalahti – tel. (9)697/51021. Jomppanen family: Tel. (9)697/57013 for booking boats, hiring canoes and renting cabins.

Park itinerary (55 km/34 miles): The traditional itinerary is partially in a loop which can be shortened by taking a motorboat up the Lemmenjoki River. The path, marked in orange, starts from the village of Njurgalahti; there are unlocked fells huts along the route, while for the detours a tent is needed.

Map: Lemmenjoki-Inari/Menesjärvi 1:50,000.

INARI

Features: Lapp center on state highway 4, in the direction of North Cape. There is a good open-air museum with a reconstruction of a Lapp village. **Fielppajärvi Church Trail** (15 km/9¼ miles outward and return): a day's trek through the forest to the old church built 1752–60, once a religious center of Lapp life, now used only a couple of times a year. The path starts about 1 km after the Lapp museum carpark.
Map: Inari-Menesjärvi 1:50,000.

URHO KEKKONEN NATIONAL PARK

Features: Opened in 1952 and and dedicated to the late Finnish president who was particularly fond of cross-country skiing, it is the second largest Finnish national park (2,550 km²/984 sq. miles), lying between the Soviet frontier and state highway No. 4.

Access and information center: The Saariselkä and Tankavaara centers are at the northern and southern edges of the park, on state highway 4, which forms the western boundary. Saariselkä Hiking Center – 99830 Saariselkä – tel (9)697/84816. Kiilopää Hiking Center – 99300 Ivalo – tel. (9)697/87101. The Tankavaara center is next to the gold museum, situated in the area of an old concession 8 km (5 miles) north of the village of Vuotso, 60 km (37 miles) south of Ivalo. **Itineraries:** There are a number of possible routes, marked in red, through a landscape of fells reaching a height of 700 m (2,300 ft). Unlocked fell huts are situated beside tracks and off the marked trails. Anyone wishing to venture into these parts should take a compass and map.
Map: Kaunispaa-Kopsusjärvi 1:50,000.

WATCH OUT FOR MOSQUITOES

These insects play a double role in maintaining the precarious ecological balance of the habitat: in an environment where finding food is a problem, they provide an important source of nourishment, especially for birds; secondly, they protect certain areas from damaging amounts of tourists. In Lapland mosquitoes have a bad reputation and their attacks on unprepared visitors can ruin a holiday. Their presence, however, is by no means predictable and their numbers fluctuate greatly from day to day according to the conditions of the weather and terrain.

For this reason it is essential, before setting out on a trek, to pack various types of mosquito repellent. Oils, sprays and mosquito wipes are generally on sale at camping sites and centers. It is important, as you go, to read the map carefully so as to distinguish tracts of wet, marshy terrain from raised, dry areas and thus prepare yourself in advance for particularly infested zones.

In Lapland, July and August are the most difficult months for mosquitoes and there is good reason why stickers with the smiling face of a mosquito bidding you welcome are cheerfully sold to tourists! However, if you can tolerate colder, more variable weather, September and the first frosts offer a dazzling wealth of autumn colours and absolutely no mosquitoes.

Opposite: detail of a dried up birch trunk still firmly rooted among the mosses of the tundra.

The pools that dot the plains of the tundra take on delicate pastel shades in the evening light.

deep in the wilderness of the park, and looking strangely isolated, stands a tiny cabin with a radio telephone, the only communication point with the outside world.

The descent into the canyon offers spectacular glimpses of the Kevo River, and crosses abrupt changes in vegetation. The walk goes through woods of birches and conifers and includes a series of easy fords (with the additional aid of a hand rail in case it is too slippery underfoot).

The sites equipped for camping are conveniently positioned and provide several welcome places to stop at during the course of the day. The one chosen as the end of this stage is on a strip of sand around a tranquil stretch of river.

From the camping site to the Utsjoki/Inari state highway   R

11.5 km (7 miles), 3/4 hours

The Kevo Canyon path continues through taiga landscape for a few kilometers and then, after the ford, climbs to a point where the conifer wood thins out leaving the terrain to low, stumpy birches.

After a last panoramic view over the Kevo from the top of the climb, the path points directly eastward. Once more you are back in the shrubby tundra with its moors and peatland, where for long stretches, among the lakes of Paldokjärvi, the route winds its way along the characteristic wooden walkways built across the marshes.

Eventually you pass a board marking the boundaries of the nature reserve and start to descend again through a pine wood. The state highway between Utsjoki and Inari is close at hand. To return to the departure point, there are local buses but these can be infrequent so check on timings prior to departure.

BEAR TRAIL

Through the taiga

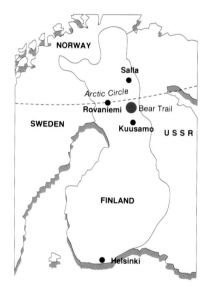

The Bear Trail, the *Karhunkierros*, from the word *karhu* which means bear in Finnish, is one of the best-known treks in Finland. It winds along the edges of Lapp territory, just south of the Arctic Circle, and not far from the frontier with the Soviet Union, while its northern section crosses part of the Oulanka National Park.

The park was created in 1956 and in 1982 its area was doubled with a proposal for further extension. It covers a typically rugged and wild part of the taiga. The landscape of the park is extremely varied with spectacular rushing rivers which cut through pine and fir forests and quieter streams that carve out their smooth and winding course in the sandy ground. Completing the beauty of the park are the roaring waterfalls, pools and marshland, silent lakes, hills that overlook vast stretches of uncontaminated nature, and finally unexpected gorges with mighty rock walls.

Numerous wooden barns, dotted along the river banks, testify to the custom in former times of gathering grass from the meadows and storing it as fodder for reindeer.

Useful addresses: Kuusamo Tourist Office (Matkailukeskus Karhuntassu) – Torangintaival 2, 93600 Kuusamo – tel. (9)89-22131; Finnish National Board of Forestry – P.O. Box 233-00121 Helsinki, 17 – tel. (9)0-61631.
Map: Rukatunturi-Oulanka 1:50,000, obtainable on the spot or in Helsinki at Karttakeskus Espa – Eteläesplanadi, 4-00130 Helsinki.
Bibliography: Pamphlets from the Finnish Tourist Board, including *Finland–Hiking Routes*.

Flora and fauna

The vegetation is typical of the taiga: in the wet forest of birch and fir, where various plants unusual in such latitudes grow, it is not always easy to walk away from the path because of the tangle of roots and

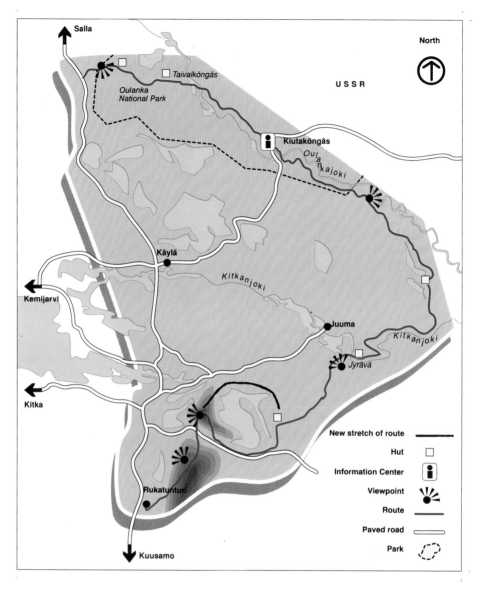

Distance: 80 km (48 miles), divided into at least four stages.
Departure point: Rukatunturi Tourist Center, 27 km (16¾ miles) north of Kuusamo; air link from Helsinki to Kuusamo then regular bus service.
Arrival point: Junction of path with state highway for Salla, 58 km (36 miles) north of Kuusamo; bus services link Kuusamo with the northern section of the trail and also with the village of Juuma, an intermediate stage.
Where to stay: Many fell huts, also called shelter cabins, along the trail. For accommodation in the southern sector there are various alternatives in Ruka and on state highway 5. In the intermediate stages, at Juuma there are the Retkietappi, Juuma and Jyrävä camping sites, with motorboat service on Lake Juuma for getting back to the Bear Trail; and at Kiutaköngäs, the Oulanka camping site.
Signposting: Marking on tree bark and rocks, white outside the bounds of the National Park, orange inside; signposts with bear symbol.
Difficulty: H = Hiker.
Equipment: Walking in Scandinavia requires clothing and equipment for protection against rain, repellents against mosquitoes and sufficient food for the entire journey.

fallen trunks. The pines that grow on the high crags, where the ground is drier, are sometimes thin and fragile, sometimes twisted by the weight of winter snow; the undergrowth is covered by a layer of mosses and lichens almost soft enough to be trodden in bare feet.

This is the territory of the great carnivores which come from the boundless wastes of the Soviet taiga. They include the bear, the wolverine (a solitary hunter) and the wolf. Often the subject of age-old legends, the wolf's presence can be detected in reality when it seeks food in winter and leaves tracks of its activities in the snow. However, you are unlikely to catch a glimpse of one along the path.

Isolated pools and marshes are the nesting grounds of wild swans and many other species of birds which find their natural habitat here: terns, ducks, wood-cocks, willow-grouse, black grouse, thrushes and numerous others, while raptors such as golden eagles, peregrine falcons, buzzards and several species of owls feed on an abundance of small rodents. The waters of the rivers (Aventojoki, Kitkanjoki, Oulankajoki and Savinajoki) and lakes, on the shores of which reindeer often drink, teem with salmon trout, perch, pike, whitefish and salmon which fight the currents and rapids.

Camping sites and cabins along the banks of the Kitkanjoki and the Oulankajoki are much frequented by the Finns who are particularly keen on fishing.

The itinerary

The *Karhunkierros*, about 80 km (48 miles) in length, does not display any marked changes in elevation but is nevertheless a taxing route which requires adequate physical preparation.

The trek begins at the tourist center of Rukatunturi, a well-known skiing resort of Finnish Lapland north of Kuusamo, and ends on the main road to Salla.

It makes no difference if you follow the trail in the opposite direction. In fact many prefer to start in the north; getting off the local bus on the road to Salla and proceeding south, simply because there are better connections back to the center of Kuusamo from Rukatunturi. In either case, however, there is a bus service connecting the departure and arrival points.

USEFUL ADVICE

When to go: For good weather July and August are the best months, although the mosquitoes can be a problem; weather conditions in September are more unpredictable but there is the compensation of marvellous autumn colours.

Clothing: In summer, around the Arctic Circle, the temperature can touch 30°C (86°F) but there is always the risk of sudden changes of weather. For this reason, in addition to normal changes of clothing for a trip of several days, it is absolutely essential to have waterproof items (ideally in gore-tex) to protect both yourself and your rucksack. Likely extremes of temperature make it advisable to cover yourself warmly at night, while during the day long trousers and long-sleeved shirts will protect the body from mosquitoes.

Equipment: Remember to take the following articles: a compass, a suitable map, insect repellents, tent, sleeping bag, camping mat, camping stove, fuel and plenty of food.

Accommodation in Finland: Apart from the option of hotels in the towns, there are plenty of unlocked fell huts (shelter cabins), locked cabins (key from tourist center), or tent sites along the trails. The Finnish campgrounds with wooden holiday cabins are ideal bases for hikers who plan to make a number of hikes during their stay. Maintained in perfect condition, they provide a comfortable place to stay. They are usually situated deep in the wood or on the lake shore, often with the chance to hire boats and canoes. Alternatively, there is the possibility of staying on a farm or hiring a private cottage.

Along the trail, the many unlocked fell huts have a stove with wood for heating and wooden boarding for sleeping, often bunk beds.

The camps, either on a lake shore or river bank, provide an area for pitching a tent, a special site for a camp fire, a wood pile and a hut with a toilet.

Above: the old Myllykowski watermill by the rapids of the Kitka River, now restored with two rooms for overnight stays.

On pages 30 and 31: the evening colours of the Far North reflected in the calm waters of Lake Juuma; view from the camping site, one of the stops along the Bear Trail.

Below: typical wooden walkways enabling walkers to cross swampy areas along the route.

The route is marked with signposts and paint on tree bark and rocks – in white outside the park bounds and in orange inside the park. At intervals all along there are shelter cabins, under a day's walk from one another. The convenient distance between these cabins and the sites suitable for pitching tents, gives hikers the opportunity to plan the duration of their trip at leisure, even though the suggestion here is to break the itinerary into four stages.

The route has recently been improved to avoid walking along the road south of Lake Porontima; our map shows the new route and the former, alternative route.

Rukatunturi to Jyrävä cabin   H

25 km (15½ miles), 8 hours

Leaving the tourist center of Rukatunturi, which in recent years, because of the construction of a number of skilifts, has undergone somewhat indiscriminate development, the first stretch follows the row of hills Ruka – Valtavaara – Konttainen; the last fells are reached after crossing the no. 8694 road leading to the village of Vuotunki. Although the ground here does not rise to more than 500 m (1,640 ft), the taiga thins out and there is a view from the top of a magnificent landscape comprising a series of lakes,

REINDEER

A first encounter with a herd of reindeer may persuade you, all things considered, that these animals, with their rather awkward gait and docile yet somewhat blank glaze, must be domesticated, even though they graze wild on the tundra and edges of the taiga. In fact, there are only a few hundred truly wild reindeer. These are larger and roam the eastern frontier with the Soviet Union. It is the presence of reindeer which makes the boundless wastes of the Far North so fascinating, reminding us of the Scandinavian origins of the legend of Father Christmas driving his sleigh over the snows of Lapland.

When winter comes, the herds leave the tundra and head southward where there are fewer problems of finding food and they can shelter from the bitter Arctic winds that rage across the taiga. In the forest they can dig more easily in the snow and find their principal source of food: lichens. When it gets warmer, they leave the humid, mosquito-infested woodlands and set off on long journeys which may prove fatal to the newborn young and in some years cause many premature deaths.

As a rule the reindeer herds, still an important resource for Lapp families, are rounded up twice a year for branding and slaughtering.

The contamination of lichens as a result of the Chernobyl nuclear disaster forced the Swedish government to kill off tens of thousands of reindeer; the decision, which was not followed by Finland and Norway (where the parameters indicating the risk threshold were perhaps higher than the Swedish), caused considerable controversy.

ORIENTATION

Trekking in Finland is often more akin to what American hikers call backpacking, which involves taking off into an area of wilderness and carrying everything you are likely to need on your back, with no chance of stocking up on the way. The presence of unlocked fell huts may do away with the necessity of carrying a tent but does not help where food is concerned. You can wander for days among the woods and lakes and the only problems will be caused by virtually inaccessible marshes and swamps. In such cases it is essential to use a compass: this is normal practice for anyone who goes hiking in Finland, as well as for any fishermen, bird-watchers and nature photographers who wish to stray from the paths and fend for themselves. But for the rambler who prefers the safety of a marked route, Finland satisfies the widest range of needs with a vast network of trails used traditionally by hunters and fishermen. In these instances the compass can remain in the rucksack but the rambler should never overlook the fact that even on a less demanding hike it is easy to lose one's sense of direction, especially in woods, where there are no points of reference. Careful observation of details, such as an anthill or moss-covered trunk and study of the daily relative position of the sun may provide useful signals as to the direction to take.

which appear as transparent specks among the darker forests below. The trail continues northwards winding between small lakes while flanking the north side of Lake Porontima. After about five hours and 14 km (8½ miles) from the departure point, you pass the old watermill on the Porontima River which today has a room that sleeps 3 to 4, providing a chance to break the journey overnight.

The path crosses an empty, partly deforested zone and then continues over boggy ground with the characteristic trunks laid as footbridges over the marshes, eventually reaching the turning for the village of Juuma.

This first stage does seem strenuous but its length is justified because there are plenty of places to stay overnight. The Jyrävä cabin (sleeps 12 on wooden

beds) faces a splendid waterfall; at Myllykoski an idyllic restored old watermill beside a suspension bridge over the rapids offers a night's stay in two dormitories, though fairly spartan without any interior heating; and the village of Juuma, a beautiful splash of colour on the lake, has camping sites, including that of Jyrävä, on the Kauhaniemi peninsula, which also offers isolated holiday cabins in the wood. The detour to Juuma is little more than a 1.5-km (1-mile) walk from Myllykoski, but you can also go to the lake by following the signs along the path and, by lowering the appropriate signal on the beach, calling in a boat to take you across the lake. At Juuma you can restock with various kinds of dried and tinned foods for the trip.

From the top of the Ristikallio cliffs there is virtually an aerial view over the loops of the Kitka River as it flows through the taiga a short distance from the Arctic Circle.

DOWN THE RAPIDS

The rivers of the Kuusamo region and in particular the Kitkanjoki and the Oulankajoki are, for enthusiasts of canoeing and rafting, among the most popular in Finnish Lapland.

The canoeist, in a setting of wild beauty, can follow the current of the Oulankajoki along a winding course that cuts through the taiga. But where a change in the level of the terrain increases the speed of the water and transforms it into raging rapids, those who are not expert can resort to organized rafting, the programmes of which vary from simple trips of a few hours to trips of several days with overnight stops.

For information apply to:

Kaylan Konttori – 93850 Kayla – tel. (9)89-41177.

Kuusamon Lomat – 93600 Kuusamo – tel. (9)89-11911.

Opposite: the Aallokkokoski rapids before the Kitka River forms the Jyrävä falls.

Below: an ideal habitat for the many birds of the Far North.

Jyrävä cabin to Jussinkämppä cabin   H

16 km (10 miles), about 6 hours

From Juuma, a loop of about 10 km (6¼ miles) (the "Little Bear Trail," marked in green) takes you on a day's ramble to see the principal attractions of the entire *Karhunkierros*: waterfalls, rapids, rivers, lakes and forests.

From Myllykoski, the Bear Trail runs alongside sandbanks, lake shores, raging rapids or the calmer waters of the Kitka River, a tributary of the Oulanka River on the border with the Soviet Union. On some stretches a number of ancient pines, uprooted by blizzards, slow up the walk through the forest thickets.

There are various sites where tents can be pitched along the river's edge and an outdoor shelter at Kahlaamo.

After Kitkanjoki (*joki* is Finnish for river) the path heads north, climbing and then bearing to the right of Lake Pesosjärvi, among pines, birch, beech and swampy ground where it is best not to stop if you are not suitably protected from the mosquitoes.

This stage ends at the Jussinkämppä cabin (sleeps 20 persons on wooden beds) on Lake Kulmakka, the calm waters of which invite you for a swim after the hard day. In fact, although situated almost at the latitude of the Arctic Circle, the summer climate here in Finland, influenced by the warm current of the Gulf Stream, is relatively mild.

Jussinkämppä cabin to Taivalköngäs cabin   H

22 km (13½ miles), about 8 hours

The former route of the *Karhunkierros* followed the shore of Lake Kulmakka but now the lake will only be open for research and not to the general public. Instead, the extension of the Oulanka National Park towards the frontier with Russia, and the construction of a new hut, allows hikers to explore a wedge of territory between the Kitka and Oulanka rivers.

From Jussinkämppä the trail heads northwards, skirting the hills to the right of the Kulmakkajärvi (*järvi* is Finnish for lake). When the first bends of the Oulankajoki appear, you are already inside the Oulanka National Park.

From above the sandbanks where reindeer bask in

The calm, quiet waters of the Oulankajoki are ideal for canoe enthusiasts.

the sun, you can sometimes see canoeists carried down on the current, following the winding course of the river.

Along the river (2¾ hours) you will find another good cabin (Ansakämppä – sleeps 10–15 on wooden beds), reached by descending a side path down a series of convenient wooden steps, and various sites fitted out for overnight stays in tents.

The route runs through pine woods, with a number of fords across small tributaries of the Oulankajoki in

FISHING TREKS

Anyone looking for the first time at a map of Finland will be surprised at the amount of blue areas which represent the country's complex system of inter-linked waterways. Finland is officially described as the land of 60,000 lakes, but a recent survey revealed that there are actually 187,888 bodies of water that qualify for that name, formed by the pressure of ice during the last Ice Age which excavated hollows and then filled them with water.

The country, therefore, is understandably a paradise for fishing enthusiasts, from quiet streams and lakes full of trout, pike, whitefish and perch to the more swiftly flowing rivers of the northern taiga where salmon abound. In order to reach the best fishing grounds anglers often have to become ramblers.

The foreign tourist must have a general fishing license to fish in Finland and this can be obtained from post offices and some holiday villages and camping sites. You also have to get a local permit for the waters in question, which are granted by local fishing associations. Two permits will cover fishing in most of this area, also obtainable from the Guide Center of the Oulanka Park.

the wet undergrowth, and then on to the series of foaming rapids of Kiutaköngäs in a gorge of granitic rock. About 1 km (⅔ mile) on from the rapids the new Guide Center of the National Park, opened in the summer of 1988, has an auditorium, an exhibition hall, a cafeteria, and further information on the itinerary. Beyond the bridge on state highway 8693, additional details of the route are provided by the Oulanka Biological Research Station.

The next section of the *Karhunkierros*, which

Above: you rejoin the Bear Trail after a halt at the village of Juuma by taking the suspension bridge over the Kurkajoki.

Below: you are likely to meet many Finnish family groups out trekking.

crosses the taiga to the Taivalköngäs cabin (sleeps 20 on wooden beds), is not very arduous and, with several delightful glimpses of the tranquil bends of the river, can be covered in a short time.

You can stop overnight in the cabin beyond the suspension bridge, with the roar of the rapids echoing below.

Taivalköngäs cabin to the road for Salla   H

9.5 km (6 miles), 3½ hours

From the Taivalköngäs cabin the route offers two alternatives: the first is the northern detour of the *Karhunkierros*, an itinerary which leads to the Oulanka Canyon (camp/cabin for 7 people) and continues, with various forks, northward along the course of the Savinajoki to Hautajärvi lake and the road to Salla (21 km/13 miles). As is clear from the map, the whole northern region of the Oulanka National Park is occupied by vast tracts of bogland, a zone strictly protected because of the number of birds that live there.

The second is the traditional itinerary which leaves the Taivalköngäs cabin and bends westward, passing the Puikkokamppa cabin (partly burnt by a fire but still usable; sleeps 10) and reaching the Aventojoki River (1½ hours) and the splendid sight of Ristikallio cliffs and gorge with its walls plunging into the river. This is a silent, peaceful spot where the pines, clinging to the rocks, are reflected in the transparent water. The cabin at Ristikallio (sleeps 10 on wooden beds) is situated above a loop in the Aventojoki which, with its calm waters, forms a lake.

This is almost the end of the journey; woods and swampy tracts lead to the junction with the road to Salla (5 km/3 miles) where, by catching the bus or organizing a lift you can return to Rukatunturi and thence to Kuusamo.

THE HOSSA REGION

Features: Protected until 1979, the Hossa region (an old Lapp village) represents the Finnish taiga landscape at its most idyllic. These are places of rare beauty – a succession of lakes linked together by a network of canals and streams. The terrain is undulating and varied, the woods dominated by pine.

Access and information center: 80 km (50 miles) south of Kuusamo on state highway 913, for information and accommodation: The Holiday Village of Hossa and the Korkeaniemi camping site are next to each other, while the Teeriranta camping site is 10 km (6¼ miles) to the north on state 913.

Itineraries over a network of about 80 km (50 km) of paths: The trails (at least eight, the longest of which is about 20 km/13 miles) criss-cross one another repeatedly and can be combined to make day-long loop trips or treks of several days' duration: in the latter instance overnight stops can be planned in huts or in the typical constructions, open on one side, known as *laavu*, dotted along the route, though it is always a good idea to take a tent. Walking in Hossa is extremely relaxing: the paths are well maintained and marked, the ground is undulating but with few changes in elevation, ideal for family trekking.

For canoeing enthusiasts the Hossa camping site is the departure point for reaching the same huts along the paths, via the complex of waterways.
Map: Hossa-Kylmäluoma 1:50,000.

THE KYLMÄLUOMA REGION

Features: The landscape is of two types, one consisting of lakes formed by high embankments of morainic origin, the other of bogland which in some places is over 3 m (10 ft) deep. At one time the grass of the wet clearings was gathered as fodder for reindeer, as witnessed by the many barns scattered through the zone.

Access and information center: The region of Kylmäluoma, near state highway 5, 50 km (31 miles) south of Kuusamo and 55 km (34 miles) west of Hossa, is linked by a daily bus service departing from the villages of Kuusamo and Taivalkoski. Accommodation and the information center are close to the Kylmäluoma camping site.
Itineraries over a 40-km (25-mile) loop: The Kylmäluoma camping site, departure point for circular hikes, is ideal for a family holiday.
Map: Hossa-Kylmäluoma 1:50,000.

PEMBROKE-SHIRE COAST PATH

Long before Wales had any need for a national park to preserve its natural beauties, folk songs of ancient local tradition celebrated that land of mystery and magic. Despite the striking contrasts with technological progress and the sometimes overwhelming pressure of summer tourism on the environment, this is still evident today in the stretch of Pembrokeshire coastline along which, for a distance of 270 km (168 miles), you can follow a footpath.

This is an ocean region of cliffs, battered by winds, and endless beaches, some of which cannot be reached at high tide. Inland the picture is of rolling upland countryside, a few scattered farms and green fields, coming down almost to the shore, where livestock graze undisturbed. Virtually all the land along the coast is privately owned and every field is hedged or fenced, part of a vast mosaic where ramblers are welcome to wander at will if they bear in mind local regulations. Even the uninitiated will be captivated by the rocks, with their diverse stratification, and delight in the sight of the spring flowers which bring colour to the cliffs in this wild region. There are hardly any coastal roads and the few that do exist drop down starkly and steeply to the shore, providing access to some remote village. Although walking the whole length of the path is a tiring and arduous enterprise, there are plenty of opportunities to choose shorter stretches which are accessible to everyone and equally interesting and beautiful.

Useful addresses: Pembrokeshire Coast National Park, County Offices, Haverfordwest, Dyfed SA61 1QZ (tel. 0437/764591).
Maps: The 3 Ordnance Survey maps 1:50,000: Landranger 158/157/145.
Bibliography: T. Roberts, *The Pembrokeshire Coast Path Guide for Walkers*, Abercastle; H. Williams, *The Pembrokeshire Coast National Park*, Webb & Bower.

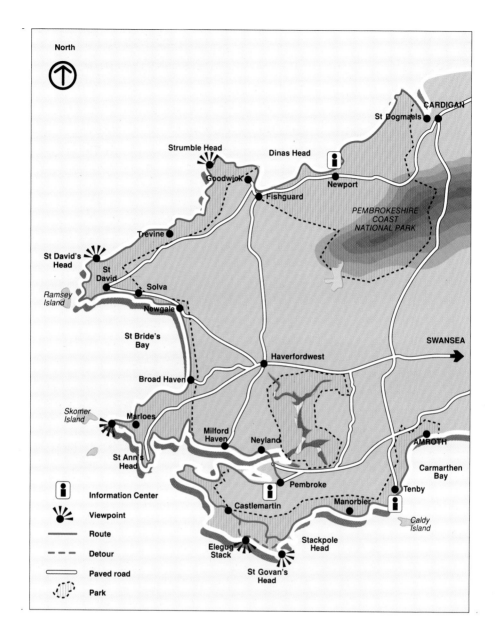

Distance: About 270 km (168 miles), divided into at least 12/14 days' walking.

Departure point: Amroth, on the southern coast of the Pembrokeshire National Park, reached by local bus from Tenby, in turn linked by several train connections towards London.

Arrival point: St Dogmael's, on the northern coast of the park near Cardigan, from there by bus to Camarthen, by train to Swansea.

Where to stay: Bed and breakfast in villages, hostels along the path and campsites (also on farms) for those who prefer to camp.

Difficulty: H = Hiker.

Signposting: Wooden placard with symbol of acorn and directional signposts.

When to go: All year round, especially spring.

Equipment: A good pair of walking shoes and something for protection against the rain; other items can be added as required; a supply of food is not necessary, water is available only in villages.

Flora and fauna

The Pembrokeshire Coast National Park is famous for the variety and abundance of its plants and animals. Not only the coast, but also the islands and the hinterland, with its wooded valleys and bleak hills, harbour a wealth of vegetable and animal life.

The climate plays an important role, offering ideal conditions for many different species to live side by side. The influence of the ocean prevents any extremes in temperature, with mild winters and cool summers which rarely register more than 16°C (61°F) along the coast.

The strident screaming of thousands of seabirds which nest in the rock clefts transform these spots into birdwatching sanctuaries. The park's emblem is the razorbill which, along with many species of gulls, lives in colonies on the islands and on the monolithic Stack Rocks facing the cliffs of the Castlemartin peninsula. Other curiosities are the puffin, with its black-and-white plumage and amazing colourful bill; the cormorant, a strong swimmer and voracious eater of fish; and the Manx shearwater, which has strange breeding habits: while one incubates underground the other feeds out to sea, returning to the nest only after night has fallen. Among the predators, the most imposing is the buzzard, while the peregrine falcon has only recently begun to repopulate the area after suffering from the use of pesticides and almost total extermination during the Second World War when official policy was to ensure the safe journey of carrier pigeons.

The most important mammal in the park is the grey seal which basks among the waves in the rock clefts and in the more inaccessible bays. There are dolphins, too, and whales swimming not far offshore. On land, foxes slink fearlessly through the fields, even in broad daylight, and more than thirty varieties of butterfly have been observed settling on flowers.

The plant life on the coast is remarkably complex: exposed to high winds and thus stripped of the trees which are to be found only in more sheltered zones, the cliffs glow with an extraordinary range of wild flowers, even during winter. But it is in spring and early summer that nature explodes in its full splendour, painting the slopes of the coastline with brilliant hues: patches of bluebells, primroses and

USEFUL ADVICE

Information on accommodation: The brochure entitled *Coast Path Accommodation*, published annually, can be found at information centers; this lists the addresses of bed and breakfast establishments, hostels and camping sites along the itinerary, with relative prices and seasonal dates of opening. Also useful is the publication *Youth Hostels on the Pembrokeshire Coast Path*.

When to go: Contrary to what happens in the mountains, where winter snow covers traces of the path, the climate of Pembrokeshire makes this path accessible throughout the year. However, May is perhaps the best month not only because of the spring flowers which soften the severity of the cliffs but also because accommodation is easier to come by than at the height of the season, especially for those without a tent.

Recommendations: The sea, like the mountains, should not be underestimated; many accidents can be avoided with a few simple precautions. These are the main safety guidelines: do not leave the path and do not venture too near the crumbly cliff edges; bear in mind that the firmness with which your shoes will adhere to rock depends on weather conditions; keep children under control on exposed stretches; remember that strong winds on cliffs are perilous; always be aware, too, that all beaches are potentially dangerous and that currents are most treacherous when the tide is coming in; never go into the water when the red flag is flying; consult the local charts giving the times of the tides so as not to risk being cut off from beach exits. Two places on the coast path, Dale and Sandy Haven, are accessible only for two hours while the tide is out; otherwise there is a 5-km (3-mile) diversion.

On pages 46 and 47: Barafundle Bay has a beautiful, fairly inaccessible sandy beach which is quiet even at the busiest times of year.

Opposite: the Neolithic dolmen of Careg Sampson, found not far from the coast at Abercastle, is a particularly well preserved example.

Manorbier Castle, on the southern stretch of the Coast Path, dates back to the Norman period (twelfth–thirteenth centuries).

heathers mingle with the clumps of bright yellow, pungently scented gorse.

The botanical diversity of the coastline is supplemented by that of the seashore itself, with the interesting ecosystem of the sand dunes, held together by the roots of pioneer plants, and the surprising variety of marine algae that can be seen growing on the rocks at low tide.

Traces of history

Nature does not provide the only interesting feature of these parts. To venture into this remote region is to tread in the footsteps of folk who for centuries, indeed from antiquity, have struggled to survive the hard ocean climate. It is the constant presence of water, that force of almost supernatural power and unpredictable temperament, which has helped to

lend these places their singular atmosphere of spiritual meaning and mystery.

The more inaccessible cliffs and nearby islands became sites of worship and meditation for ascetics and monastic communities when, in the fifth and sixth centuries, Christianity spread through Britain. Numerous chapels, built along the shore and dedicated to saints of the Celtic church, were places of prayer for seamen. Later, the Roman Catholic church absorbed them. Many, now in ruins, are hidden among the bushes, others stand solitary in the face of the wind. Among the latter is St Govan's Chapel, from the thirteenth century (the cell cut into the rock and the altar are much older), the origins of which are shrouded in legend and mystery. St David's peninsula, with its steep cliffs and tiny bays, was used as a landing place for pilgrims, becoming a focus of Christianity for medieval society and a cen-

ter of pilgrimage second only to Rome. Legend tells of St David, patron saint of Wales, who built his monastery on the spot where the cathedral stands today, not far from the ruins of the episcopal palace, in a position well concealed from the Vikings, then the awesome predators of the seas. And if this corner of land still breathes a profound spirit of holiness in the way of life and local customs, one can only reflect on what mystic sensations inspired the symbols of even more ancient religious beliefs, such as the famous Neolithic dolmens scattered at intervals all along the coast.

As a result of the Norman occupation, from the eleventh century onward, many castles were built along this coastline, and the regions to the north with

Animals grazing inland in peaceful rural surroundings; the rugged coastline, along which the path winds, is just visible in the background.

their strongly Welsh allegiances were divided from the south, more wedded to English traditions. The imaginary line of this frontier helped to separate the two provinces whose differences in language, culture and even architecture are evident to this very day, although the adoption of bilingual nomenclature throughout Pembrokeshire has partially lessened these distinctions.

In the following centuries, while agriculture was concentrated in the hinterland, political unity with England (1536) stimulated trade between the coastal villages and the continent. Yet again the sea played a fundamental role in the lives of the Welsh people: they exported wool and livestock, brought coal from inland areas, and mined limestone along the south

THE MYSTERY OF THE PAST

The most ancient signs of human presence in Pembrokeshire date back more than 20,000 years when primitive man, still a hunter, made his home in caves. The first to cultivate the land and start raising livestock were our Neolithic ancestors, about 5,000 years ago, traces of whom have survived principally in the dolmens, mysterious and imposing burial chambers which are to be found scattered all over the plateau. Among the best preserved examples are the dolmens of Pentre Ifan, on the northern edge of the Presely Hills, and of Careg Sampson, not far from the coast, near Abercastle. Often the legendary heroes after whom some of the dolmens are named increase the speculation as to the origins of these monuments, still the subject of conflicting theories. The most intriguing suggestion is that Neolithic man transported eighty stones, each weighing about four tonnes, from the hills of Pembrokeshire down to Stonehenge on Salisbury Plain. A link has been discovered in certain samples of volcanic rock with rock found only in the Presely Hills. Another interesting theory is that the stones were carried down naturally by glaciers during the last Ice Age.

At the dawn of the third millennium B.C. the afforestation process begun by Neolithic farmers was speeded up by the introduction of metal tools in the Bronze and Iron Ages. The new inhabitants of the coastal lands, who had come, like their ancestors, from overseas, exploited the defensive possibilities of the cliffs by raising embankments and digging trenches to form compact settlements at the head of promontories in order to protect their tribal communities from the enemy and to provide shelter from storms; typical Iron Age fortifications such as these are to be found at many points along the Coast Path but by now are difficult to distinguish from natural depressions if you do not look carefully.

THE EFFECT OF EROSION

The Pembrokeshire coast offers wonderful opportunities to ornithologists and botanists; and for geologists, too, this tightly confined region is of exceptional interest because of the incredible variety of rocks and multiform stratifications that make up the cliffs. Although the volcanic rocks of the northern section go back more than 2,000 million years, the modern appearance of the coastal plateau is explained by much more recent geological events: it is the destructive action of the sea, combined with the erosive force of the water which melted after the last Ice Age, that have shaped the present landscape.

When Atlantic storms exert pressure on the cliffs, mainly threatening their base, the type of erosive action is determined by the solidity of the rock. The repetitive pattern of alternating promontories and bays, so evident in the coastal stretch from St David's Head to Strumble Head, is caused by the contrasting effects of erosion on the harder volcanic strata and on the softer sedimentary rock. Similarly, the development of caves, natural arches and monolithic rocks (de-

rived from the crumbling of the arches themselves) on the cliffs from St Govan's Head to Elegug Stacks in the southern sector of the Coast Path, has come about as a result of the particular solubility of limestone rock in water. Along the beaches, on the other hand, where the water is relatively calmer, conditions are ripe for the accumulation of marine sediments and eroded material from the cliffs.

Apart from the eroding action of the ocean, in recent geological times water melted from glaciers has also shaped the landscape. During the last Ice Age, in fact, the solidification of water into enormous blocks of ice notably lowered the present level of the sea and the rivers cut deep trenches into the valleys; but when the average temperature rose once more, the environment was subjected to the opposite effect of flooding as a result of the thaw. A classic example of this phenomenon is the river basin of the port of Milford Haven and, on a smaller scale, of Sova, both disproportionate to the actual volume of their rivers.

coast which was heated and spread as fertilizer.

This type of activity ceased with the arrival of the industrial age and the railways, ushering in the modern era with all its complex problems, not the least of which has been the contrasting impact of progress on the one hand and preservation of the environment on the other.

The itinerary

Laid out in 1953 as the natural consequence of the setting up of the park, the Coast Path was only opened in 1970 as it took that many years to bring such an ambitious project to fruition. Consisting to a large extent of privately owned coastal land, it was not always easy to obtain permission from the individual landlords for it to be used as a public thoroughfare. Gates left open, animals disturbed and crops trampled underfoot were among the arguments cited, not always wrongly, in opposition to the path which has now become a reality.

The signposts with the acorn symbol which mark the route.

Despite the oil refineries of the neighbouring zones of Pembroke and Milford Haven and the artillery range on the Castlemartin peninsula (which forces ramblers to take an irritating detour inland), the major part of the itinerary runs through wild and beautiful scenery, with many traces of the past making it a real journey of discovery. The dominating element, forever changing its mood, is the ocean, which has never ceased to exercise its influence, not only on the local plant and animal life, but also on man and his works – villages, tiny harbours, castles and the like. Except for the above-mentioned industrial area, the walk is almost exclusively along a path, on the beaches when the tide is out or occasionally on the road through villages.

It is possible to make diversions inland by branching off on footpaths, which interconnect and lead back to the main path.

The whole journey can easily be done in 12 to 14 days but may take longer if stops have to be made for bad weather or if trips are taken to islands offshore.

If you have less time to spare, the stretch from Castlemartin to St Ishmael's, beyond Milford Haven, can conveniently be omitted, so avoiding the refineries of the most heavily built-up area in Pembrokeshire.

The planning of the various stages and the physical

The cemetery and church of Manorbier on the southern tract of the Coast Path; apart from the natural features along the trail, there are many places of worship and religious monuments which all point to the spiritual history of this religious land.

preparation for the walk are matters of individual choice. In the following description of the itinerary we have adopted a simple geographical subdivision, suggesting overnight stops as and when appropriate for each section of the route.

THE SOUTH COAST

Amroth to Milford Haven   H

91 km (57 miles), 4/5 days
Overnight stays: Amroth/Saundersfoot; Tenby and neighbourhood; Manorbier; Freshwater East; Castlemartin; Pembroke; Milford Haven.

This section of the route, excluding the crossing of the urban area of Pembroke and Milford Haven, is the most popular. Despite the numbers of people, you can walk for long stretches in complete solitude and the limestone cliffs of the Castlemartin peninsula, with arches, caves and jutting rocks, provide some of the most spectacular views of the entire journey.

Leave from the Norman castle of Amroth; on the beach at low tide there are occasional traces of fossils from a forest submerged more than 7,000 years ago. Between Wiseman's Bridge and Saundersfoot, which emerged as a port as a result of its anthracite mines in the nineteenth century, the Coast Path follows the track of the old railway that remained functional until the closing of the last mine in 1939.

The tourist village of Tenby, which is very busy in high season, was a summer resort in the Victorian age; from here boats leave for Caldey, the island of Cistercian monks.

Before proceeding further it is advisable to find out beforehand the times of artillery exercises at Giltar Point; the road inland is closed when the firing ranges are in use and the red flag is flying. Once back on the path, with views of hidden coves and steep cliffs, you pass the Priest's Nose point, at the eastern tip of Manorbier Bay, with the Neolithic dolmen of King's Quoit.

At Manorbier you can visit the private castle built in the twelfth and thirteenth centuries, open to the public from April to October.

On the other side of Freshwater East, which has undergone extensive tourist development, the undulating red sandstone cliffs give way, at Greenala

THE PEMBROKESHIRE NATIONAL PARK

The Pembrokeshire National Park, opened in 1952, is the smallest of such parks in Britain. Although situated almost entirely along the south coast of Wales, the various inland sections should not be overlooked, for their varied landscape offers plenty of interest to walkers: the wooded valleys of the Daucleddau surrounding the Cleddau, Carew and Cresswell river basins, and the desolate slopes of the Presely Hills in the highest part of the coastal plateau.

The administrators of the park had to face many complex problems, both inside and outside its bounds, in order to maintain the delicate balance, essential for proper management, between conservation of the environment and the basic needs of the local people. First and foremost there had to be full collaboration and agreement with the rural population, which owned 90 per cent of the land, to compensate them for the scrapping of farming programmes.

The park authorities are moreover responsible for safeguarding the particularly fragile environment against the ever-growing pressures of tourism: one example is that of the sand dunes, which are worn away by continuous trampling, destroying the protective layer formed by numerous pioneer plants.

Such problems reflect the wishes of the local people and the needs of outside visitors, but pressures on a national level also weigh upon the park's future: more than 6,000 acres of land are still reserved for military training purposes. Although it may seem inconceivable that in a protected area there should be space granted for such activities, some environmentalists actually maintain that the presence of the army guarantees the integrity, for the benefit of seabirds, of a vast habitat that might otherwise be jeopardized if given over to agriculture.

Undoubtedly the most violent impact on the park in recent years has been the development of the oil industry in and around the built-up areas of Pembroke and Milford Haven. Yet despite a number of incidents of ecological pollution, some of them serious, which have occurred along the coast in the past few decades, the discovery of new deposits in the North Sea have markedly reduced the volume of maritime traffic from the Persian Gulf and the dangers that once seemed likely to imperil the preservation of the natural environment would appear partly to have been averted.

Although the Coast Path, on the outer edge of the park, has to skirt the vast oil plants, it has to be admitted that they are found in the most highly populated area of Pembrokeshire and that walkers can, if they wish, miss out the whole area and take up the more unspoiled stretch of the path on the other side of Milford Haven.

Cows grazing peacefully on the seashore are a familiar sight.

On pages 58 and 59: the Strumble Head lighthouse, on the northern stretch of the walk, is strategically situated on the coast facing Ireland.

Point, to vertical limestone formations of the Carboniferous period.

Beyond Stackpole Quay, owned by the National Trust, Barafundle Bay is a quiet spot, uncrowded even in summer because of its comparative inaccessibility.

Behind the dunes of the splendid beach at Broad Haven, the Bosherston Pools offer an alternative route to the Coast Path when the guns are firing on the Castlemartin peninsula; and in the middle of the bay Church Rock, jutting out of the sea, is the remains of an ancient eroded cliff.

West of St Govan's Cape you can descend by a flight of stone steps to St Govan's Chapel, set in a rock cleft.

In the next stretch of coastline, arches, rocks and

deep sinkholes, where the sound of the sea's under-tow echoes through underground caves, form spectacular changes of scene. The vertical wall of Huntsman's Leap is so sheer it could be a training ground for freeclimbers; and the rocks known as Elegug Stags, home of sea birds, form an enormous natural arch – the so-called Green Bridge of Wales – carved by the erosive action of the sea.

Public access to these natural marvels, however, is not always permitted (east of Elegug Stacks, unless on a guided tour, the coastline is permanently closed to walkers) because of the artillery exercises over the entire Castlemartin peninsula, one of NATO's most important training areas. But when the guns are quiet (as is usually the case on bank holidays, information being given in the local papers and by the National Park offices) you can follow the path from St Govan's Chapel to Elegug Stacks, where you then have to branch off inland on the road to Castlemartin. The coast path is rejoined at Freshwater West. At the southern end of the beach (dangerous for swimmers) is the last example of a hut used for drying seaweed.

On the far side of the Angle peninsula there are fortified ruins from various wars, testifying to the strategic importance of this bay; then the path leaves the confines of the park and leads to the built-up areas of Pembrokeshire and the sharply contrasting modern oil refineries. Apart from a few sights of historic note, such as the Norman castle of Pembroke, the rest of the route, to the other side of Milford Haven, has few points of great interest.

THE WEST COAST

Milford Haven to Solva   H

69 km (43 miles), 3 days
Overnight stays: Marloes; Broad Haven; Solva.

The Dale peninsula with St Ann's Head encloses the long, narrow bay of Milford Haven and walkers skirting the bay's edge can turn their backs on the disfiguring and disruptive features – the military zones and industrial complexes – of the previous days.

From St Ann's lighthouse on a rock buffeted by Atlantic breakers, there are marvellous views. At Marloes Sands, one of the loveliest of all the local

THE ISLANDS OF THE NATIONAL PARK

If you want to interrupt the coastal trek, the islands of the park, which you can glimpse from the cliffs as you walk, offer a delightful alternative. Their names, clearly of Scandinavian origin, represent the only trace of the Vikings who, between the ninth and eleventh centuries, braved these currents and tides in their longships.

Now uninhabited, with one exception, they provide naturalists with an extraordinary opportunity to study the countless birds which nest here, lending added enchantment to this landscape. Though barren and devoid of shrubs and trees, it is even more beautified by the multicoloured ranks of wild flowers which bloom with vigour in spring and summer.

The islands of Caldey and Skomer are the most accessible, and a regular boat service operates from Easter to the end of summer.

Caldey Island, south of Tenby, is inhabited by a community of Cistercian monks who farm and make scents from wild lavender and gorse.

Skomer Island, off the Dale and Marloes peninsulas, was inhabited until 1958; the numerous colonies of seabirds are of particular interest to ornithologists. Grey seals can often be seen splashing in the waves or basking on the rocks at low tide.

Skokholm Island, just south of Skomer, is the site of the first bird observatory in Britain, set up by the naturalist R. M. Lockley in 1939.

Grassholm Island is the farthest from the coast.

Ramsey Island is separated from the mainland (St David's peninsula) by a tide race; its beaches are an ideal refuge for female grey seals in the gestation period.

Gateholm Island, once the center of an old monastic community, is accessible at low tide from the western end of Marloes Sands.

beaches, you can admire The Three Chimneys, sedimentary rock walls dating from the Silurian period (400 million years ago), the vertical layers of which have been subjected to violent telluric pressure.

The islands of Skomer and Skokholm, once inhabited and today only bird sanctuaries, can be reached by boat from Martins Haven, while Gateholm, with its many archaeological finds, is accessible on foot at low tide.

Near the small landing stage of St Bride's Haven, well sheltered from the winds, the church and cemetery, which date back to the earliest period of Christianity, are situated at the foot of green meadows descending to the sea. Before the village of Little Haven, the Coast Path unexpectedly plunges into a dense wood of oak, ash, hazelnut and blackthorn growing on the slopes by the shore, which makes a pleasant change. It then crosses a broad area covered with gorse to reach the great beach of Newgale, flanked by a huge wall of pebbles which Atlantic storms have thrown up over the centuries. In the next tract of rugged coastline which leads to the picturesque little harbour of Solva, the alternation of coves and promontories clearly illustrates the diverse geological nature of the rock strata shaped by the erosive force of the ocean.

THE NORTHERN COAST

Solva to St Dogmael's   H

112 km (70 miles), 5/6 days
Overnight stays: St David's; Trevine; Pwllderi; Fishguard; Newport; St Dogmael's.

Following in the footsteps of the medieval pilgrims, branch off the path to the inland town of St David's, in the heart of St David's peninsula and for centuries a very important spiritual center. In the cathedral the relics of St David are kept, while many testaments to early Christianity are to be found along the coast: the well and ruins of the chapel of St Non, mother of the saint; Porth Stinian, an old landing place for pilgrims; and Whitesand Bay, ideal for surfing, with dunes that conceal the chapel of St Patrick, patron saint of Ireland who, according to legend, set sail from here to convert the inhabitants of that island.

GERMANY

RED DEER TRAIL

Along the paths of the Black Forest

The Black Forest, so named because of the dark colour of its firs, is a mountain chain which extends in a north to north-easterly direction for about 150 km (93 miles) in the state of Baden-Württemberg.

It is bounded to the west by the Rhine, rising steeply from it; to the east it descends gradually to the Neckar valley and the plain that separates it from the Swabian Alps.

Its origins are older than those of the Alpine chain, dating back to the Hercynian folding which reached its climax 320 million years ago and was subsequently levelled off by atmospheric agents.

The Black Forest takes the form of a series of gentle undulations of modest average height: 700 m (2,300 ft) in the northern sector of the Kinzig River where sandstone and limestone predominate (the highest peak is the Hörnisgrinde, 1,494 m/4,900 ft); and 1,000 m (3,200 ft) in the south, characterized by granite massifs (the highest peaks are the Feldberg, 1,495 m/4,904 ft and the Belchen, 1,415 m/4,641 ft).

After the last shaping process by glaciers during the Quaternary, the present morphology of the region has mainly been caused by the eroding action of rivers which have deepened the pre-existing valleys and cut out new ones (Wütach and Gauchach), isolating the highlands and making the landscape look more irregular than its modest altitude would suggest.

The number of watercourses is also due to the special atmospheric conditions of the region, open as

Useful addresses: Kurverwaltung Freudenstadt, Postfach 440, 7290 Freudenstadt, tel. (0)7441/60.74.
Maps: Auf der Fährte des Rothirsches 1:50,000, available from the Tourist Board of Freudenstadt. More detailed, but without the itinerary marked, are the Kompass maps 1:30,000, pages 877–8. Also, the Spazier und Wanderkarte 1:20,000 with the Schwarzenberg and Schönmünzach routes.
Bibliography: There are guides to treks available on the spot.

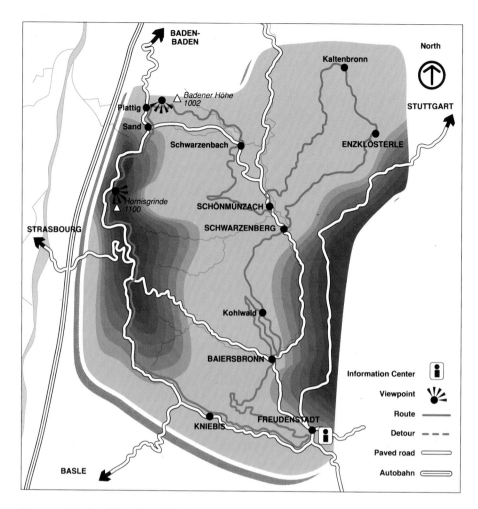

Distance: 145 km (90 miles), divided down into ten stages.
Departure and arrival points: Freudenstadt, a picturesque little town situated in a panoramic position 50 km (31 miles) from Baden-Baden, to which it is linked by the Schwarzwald Hochstrasse. It can be reached from the south along the Basel-Karlsruhe autobahn, taking the Appenweier exit.
Where to stay: Stages 2, 3, 9 and 10 end in villages where it is possible to choose from hotels, guest houses or rooms in private homes with bed and breakfast service. The other stages, however, terminate at isolated hotels (often de

luxe). Along the itinerary there are numerous guest houses and at principal junctions in the woods unlocked huts provide emergency shelter.
Signposting: The official sign is a blue diamond on a square white background. Another is a diamond sign with the drawing of a deer in green. On the map the Red Deer route is indicated by a continuous green line. This does not always correspond exactly with the signposts along the way. When the itinerary coincides with the Mittelweg (stage 3) and the Westweg (stages 6, 7, 8 and 9), a red diamond replaces the blue one.

Difficulty: R. The trek is exclusively along forest tracks closed to traffic; they are sometimes paved but are more often mud tracks which over some stretches become paths. In any event they are easily negotiated. The abundance of other signs indicating local footpaths and the number of intersecting forest tracks may sometimes lead to errors, particularly as there are no reference points deep inside the woods. It is as well, therefore, to be provided with a map and compass.
When to go: April/May and September/October.
Equipment: Mid-mountain.

it is to the influx of major fronts from the west and north and therefore subject to heavy rainfall which sometimes takes the form of snow.

As a result the ridges of the Black Forest are the sources of many tributaries of the Rhine to the south and the Neckar to the north, while the Breg and the Brigach flow eastward, coming together at Donaueschingen to form the Danube.

As for plant species, the Black Forest has changed its natural vegetation many times over the centuries according to human pressures, and today conifers (firs and pines) prevail over broad-leaved trees. Small areas have been declared *Bannwälder* (reserved wood) where all human access is prohibited.

The Black Forest in history

The first human settlements were outside the Black Forest proper and even today the most important cities are situated on its outskirts: Freiburg to the west in the Rhine Valley and Donaueschingen to the east.

Small villages linked to the agrarian economy and, from the eighteenth century, associated with the clockmaking craft, sprang up inside the forest. The most typical settlement was therefore a large, isolated, self-sufficient farm, generally built on a gentle slope; these are enormous buildings on a rectangular plan, with a wooden framework and a steeply sloping roof which is hipped and scaled.

There are seven different types of farmhouse but the common denominator was the building of the stable, hay loft and granary alongside the living quarters so that they were easily accessible in winter without having to go outside. Some farmhouses also have a balcony at the front or a door on all sides.

Agriculture was mainly a feature of the central and southern parts of the Black Forest. To the north the forest still retains its very compact appearance but every corner of it is accessible thanks to a dense network of roads; hundreds of kilometers are closed to motor traffic and negotiable only on foot. In the center and south, on the other hand, there are broad clearings, cultivated fields and residual woods, the result of recent replantings, laid out in a series of geometrically patterned areas.

In modern times tourist activity has taken precedence over the traditional activities of farming,

THE AGE OF THE EUROPEAN MOUNTAINS

The European mountain chains, the ideal environment for trekking, exhibit marked morphological differences, ranging from the gentle undulations of the Black Forest in Germany or of the Finnish tundra to the jagged icy peaks of the Western Alps and the rock fortresses of the Dolomites. In fact they originated in different geological eras and have therefore been eroded by the climate to a different extent.

The formation of the mountains of Europe dates back to the Paleocene when two major movements were registered: the older was the Caledonian which reached a climax about 430 million years ago, in the Silurian, following the drawing together of the Canadian and Baltic shields.

Remains of the Caledonian chain can nowadays be found in Greenland, in North America (Appalachians), in Britain and in Scandinavia, taking the form of huge mounds known as "old red sandstone." The chain, in fact, broke up as a result of continental drift and external forces continued, in a desert climate, the dismantling work.

The second orogenetic movement of the Paleozoic reached its peak about 320 million years ago. This especially affected North America, central Asia, Antarctica and Europe where the remains of Hercynian massifs form the skeleton of the continent. The great Hercynian ranges which once extended from the Spanish Meseta to the Urals were levelled by degradation down to the bed. As a result of successive foldings, the latter underwent further processes of lowering and uplifting. In the first case they formed depressions, in the second the beds were raised more than 1,000 m (3,200 ft) along the major fracture lines and their peaks today constitute the Massif Central and Vosges in France, the Black Forest in Germany and the Mittelgebirge mountains of Germany and Czechoslovakia.

THE MAJOR THOROUGHFARES OF THE BLACK FOREST

The Black Forest Association has signposted hundreds of kilometers of road in this region which makes it possible to undertake lengthy treks or circular tours.

The most famous west–east thoroughfare is the Querweg (transverse path). Opened in 1934, this itinerary links the city of Freiburg with Lake Constance and can be walked in seven easy stages. The most interesting sectors are undoubtedly the first and the middle parts through the Wütach gorges. Beyond Singen, on the other hand, which is outside the Black Forest, the country is more heavily populated and roads replace the forest paths and tracks.

From north to south there are three major signposted itineraries. The Westweg (western path), 280 km (174 miles), links Pforzheim and Basel by way of Interzarten and Feldberg. The Mittelweg (central path) also starts at Pforzheim and runs 233 km (145 miles) to Waldshut in the Rhine Valley. The Ostweg (eastern path) is 238 km (148 miles) long and links Pforzheim with Schaffhausen in Switzerland.

The Black Forest is also crossed from north to south by the European Long-Distance Footpath E 1 which runs from the North Sea (Flensburg) to the Adriatic (Genoa) and which coincides for several stages with the Westweg.

For the most part, all the above-mentioned itineraries are along forest tracks with short stretches on paths.

On pages 61, 64 and 65: the Black Forest presents an ever varying landscape of green hills, dense fir woods and meadows.

Right: some of the old farmhouses are surprisingly large. Many now have been turned into hotels and lodgings to meet the tourist demands of today.

forestry and local crafts. Many towns have been developed as summer and winter holiday resorts. In the north, along the famous Schwarzwald Hochstrasse which links Baden-Baden to Freudenstadt, there are short ski runs and lifts. In the south the most important tourist centers are Interzarten and Titisee-Neustad, at the foot of the Feldberg mountains, with their chairlifts and ski slopes.

The itinerary

There are several circular marked trails in the Black Forest which lead to the places of greatest interest and beauty. The most northerly trek, described here, covers a loop of 145 km (90 miles) through some of the most unspoiled, least populated woodland areas.

This is called the Red Deer Trail, named after the most typical forest animal which can be seen grazing in the many reserves en route.

The trail is largely over forest tracks which are strictly closed to normal traffic, and for some stretches on paths. The roads criss-cross one another so frequently that the itinerary can be varied accord-

ing to individual choice, provided you carry a good map. The route listed here is the standard one, divided into ten stages. Walkers with a minimum of training can do it easily in eight stages, combining, say, the sixth and seventh and the ninth and tenth.

Freudenstadt to Baiersbronn R

12 km (7½ miles), 3 hours, change in elevation 100 m (320 ft) uphill, 150 m (480 ft) downhill

The itinerary begins on the west side of the town, descending towards the Christophstal valley (deer enclosure) below and continuing along a series of forest roads high above the valley floor. Past the Sandwaldhütte, it reaches the Sankenbachwasserfall. You now leave the road and descend an artificial path with steps beside the waterfall. The scenery is delightful but the falls are only to be seen when the river's sluiceway is open. At the foot of the falls is Lake Sankenbach. Here, you again join the path leading down the entire valley to the carpark (deer enclosure) and the village of Baiersbronn below (hotels, guest houses, bed and breakfast).

THE SOURCES OF THE DANUBE

The Danube originates at the confluence of the Brigach and Breg streams, but which of the two is the true source is still a matter of debate among geographers. Tradition, in fact, locates the sources of the Danube in the park of the castle of Donaueschingen where a fountain was built, surmounted by the statue of a woman representing the river itself. The water from the fountain spurts into the Brigach just beneath its confluence with the Breg. However, because the geographical situation of the source of a river is always as far upstream as possible, arguments were put forward for the candidacy of the Breg, which has its origins in the district of Furtwangen near Martinskapelle. The debate is not easily resolved, either: the sources of the Danube are an important tourist attraction and the two villages obviously have a vested interest.

Baiersbronn to Schwarzenberg   R

16 km (10 miles), 4 hours, change in elevation about 250 m (820 ft) uphill, 300 m (985 ft) downhill

From Baiersbronn continue towards Tonbach but turn left at the Gasthof Brücke and make a steep climb up the western side of Mount Häslen. Take the road through the wood (Z 13) to the junction with the Z 19 route, climbing the valley to Hasengrund. You now descend the Tonbach valley to the village of Kohlwald (Hotel Tanne, de luxe category) and continue through attractive scenery along the marked path beside the torrent as far as the deer reserve. Go round the enclosure and on the opposite slope of the valley climb up to the road leading to Tonbach. Make sure, after about 400 m (¼ mile), to turn left and make a short climb to the road signposted Z 21 which looks down on Lake Huzenbacher (viewpoint), passes a number of huts and then descends to the village of Schwarzenberg (you can stay at the de luxe Hotel Sackmann or in one of the local guest houses).

Schwarzenberg to Enzklösterle   R

15 km (9¼ miles), 4 hours, change in elevation 360 m (1,180 ft) uphill, 285 m (935 ft) downhill

The steep paved road out of the village leads to meadows where you must pay careful attention to the many signposts (with figure of deer) so as to avoid straying off on local paths. You then enter into thick forest and climb to the top of a wide ridge with a hut. This is the intersection with the Mittelweg (the central path of the Black Forest) which runs down to Freudenstadt. You now begin a long descent of the opposite slope of the ridge, partly on the road, partly by way of steep and more direct shortcuts, down to the gulley of the Kaltembach river and the attractive Kaltembach lake. At this point keep to the left side of the valley and continue along the road to the village of Gompelscheuer. Cross the road and take the left-hand path (closed to traffic) which runs parallel but above it, to the right of the Grosse Enz river. Continuing just over 3 km (2 miles) to the north-east you reach the charming little town of Enzklösterle (hotels, guest houses, bed and breakfast).

ACID RAIN

While walking through the Black Forest you are bound to come across information cards explaining the phenomenon of acid rain and its repercussions on the forest ecosystem.

The forest is situated on the edges of two major European industrial areas, those of the Rhine and the Ruhr, and consequently sulphur dioxide wastes are concentrated in the air currents directly over the Black Forest.

This produces the phenomenon of acid rain because when sulphur dioxide comes into contact with rain water, it is transformed into sulphuric acid. This harms the plants making them gradually shed their leaves, turn yellow and die.

The first symptoms of the trouble were recorded in the seventies in Bavaria, Baden-Württemberg and in northern Rhineland-Westphalia. Among the species most affected were the common silver fir and the Norway spruce.

It is estimated that in Germany almost 8 per cent of the woodland area (600,000 hectares/1,480,000 acres) may already have been seriously damaged, but the German Forest Association claims that about 2,000,000 hectares/4,800,000 acres) of conifers are diseased as a result of acid rain.

According to the B.U.N.D. (the German League for the Environment and Protection of Nature), the Black Forest is in a sense the epicenter of the phenomenon; should it continue at the same rate, the whole forest will be wiped out during the next century.

Opposite: the church and small cemetery of the village of Schwarzenberg, a characteristic corner of the Black Forest where you can stop on the Red Deer Trail.

On page 71: overnight stops give you a chance to savour something of village life; by day, however, you are on your own amid the silence of the forest and its hidden lakes.

CROSS-COUNTRY SKIING

In spite of its low altitude, the Black Forest does have a modest amount of snowfall in the winter months which makes its gentle mountain slopes ideal terrain for cross-country skiing.

The official ski trail, signposted throughout, is 100 km (62 miles) long and links Schönach in the north (870 m/2,880 ft) with Belchen-Multen in the south (1,010 m/3,313 ft), by way of Hinterzarten and the Feldberg (1,495 m/4,904 ft). The total change in elevation is 1,500 m (4,920 ft) uphill and 1,000 m (3,280 ft) downhill. The most comfortable way to tackle it is in three stages: Schönach-Neukirch (via the sources of the Breg and the Brend viewpoint): Neukirch-Hinterzarten (890 m/2,919 ft): and Hinterzarten-Feldberg-Belchen Multen. The hardest climb is the one from Rinken to the top of the Feldberg, but the rest of the route consists of gentle ups and downs. There are many inns along the trail.

The Tourist Office at Schönach distributes a map that shows the whole ski trail. More detailed information is available on the 1:50,000 scale Wintersportkarte, Schwarzwald Mitte and Schwarzwald Sud (Schwarzwald-vereins, Rathausgar, 33, Freiburg; the main tracks are signposted with a series of red dots).

Enzklösterle to Schönmünzach   R

22 km (13¾ miles), 5½ hours, change in elevation 380 m (1,245 ft) uphill, 450 m (1,475 ft) downhill

This is one of the most tranquil stages, almost entirely through woods, with no villages or intermediate resting points. From Enzklösterle you head north-west around the edge of a large deer enclosure, after which there is a long, steady ascent towards the Kaltenbronn. The last stretch before the pass consists of a climb, with fine views, up a bare slope, muddy after rain. Prior to reaching the Kaltenbronn, an unmarked road on the left leads directly to the junction with the return path, just below the Hohlohsee (this is the route marked on the map). If you need to make a stop, however, continue following the Red Deer signs and you will come to the Kaltenbronn pass (accessible by road; skilift; bar-restaurant); you can then climb back up a steep track to the Hohlohsee. The lake is in the middle of a lovely natural reserve set up to protect this swampy area. The path along the left shore is on a wooden walkway leading through dwarf pines to the Prinzenhütte where it crosses the roads of the Westweg (western path) that lead directly to Forbach (south-west) and the Mittelweg. The Red Deer itinerary follows the latter which heads south, passing the viewpoint of the Toter Man (915 m/3,000 ft), the plateau of Schramberg and the Blockhaus. About 1 km (⅔ mile) beyond the hut, leave the Mittelweg on your left and head right on the Kaltenbachweg to the Aschenrank hut. After 500 m (500 yards) turn left on the Schellweg to Schönmünzach (hotels, guest houses, bed and breakfast).

Schönmünzach to Schwarzenbach Hotel   R

17 km (10½ miles), 5 hours, change in elevation 320 m (1,050 ft) uphill

From the town park follow the forest road that ascends north-west to Schurmsee, a lake set deep in the wood (local signposts T 6a, R 45 and R 47). This is the beginning of the most complicated stretch of the itinerary because of the maze of possible routes. A steep path on the right shore of the lake leads up diagonally to the Schurmhöne-Vordere Langeck (956 m/3,135 ft). Here, take another forest track on the right which drops down to the south-east. After less than 1 km (⅔ mile) there is a narrow park branching off on the left. After another 200 m (200 yards) you will find another shortcut which brings you to the route, followed in the Z 11 itinerary, from Schönmünzach to the Rohrgrundhütte and down to the valley of Erbersbronn (accessible by road; Grüner Wald bar-restaurant).

Cross this road and climb through meadows past the house below on the right and turn left on a well-marked forest track which climbs diagonally to Steinbruchweg; bear left again and finally branch right down to the shores of the big artificial lake of Talsperre.

Schwarzenbach Hotel to Plattig   H

12 km (7½ miles), 4 hours, change in elevation 330 m (1,082 ft) uphill

From the hotel, cross the dam and head north-westward. Turn right at the signposted junction and then left (Red Deer signs) for a road which climbs above the wood to meet the Westweg and the European Long-Distance Footpath E 1 which from now on coincides with our itinerary. After some 3 km (1¾

THE BLACK FOREST WITHOUT A RUCKSACK

The Freudenstadt Tourist Board, together with the Black Forest Association, accepts advance booking of rooms in hotels at the various stages and arranges for the transport of baggage.

To utilize this service, write to the Board with details of your proposed trip, the days when you intend to be staying at the various places and the type of service you require. Transport of baggage from one hotel to another is free of charge.

The hotels participating in this scheme are: Kurhotel Sonne (Freudenstadt); Kurhotel Tanne (Tonbach); Hotel Sackmann (Schwarzenberg); Waldhom Post (Enzklösterle); Kurhotel Schwarzwald (Schönmunzach); Schwarzenbach Hotel (Talsperre); Kurhaus Buhlerhone (Plattig); Hotel Mummelsee; Hotel Schliffkopf; Hotel Waldlick (Kniebis).

miles) the road ends at Lake Herrenweiser, which is the starting point for one of the most interesting stretches of the entire trek. Take the path which twists its way up to the Seekopf (1,001 m/3,283 ft), the most beautiful viewpoint over the artificial lake below. Proceed along a wide, level ridge to the Badener Höne (1,002m/3,286 ft), a platform with a hut and high stone viewing tower. Then descend a footpath leading to the Herrenwieser saddle. The European Footpath E 1 and the Westweg continue left towards Sand. However, the Red Deer itinerary (unmarked) is to the right and leads down to Plattig after passing the Schuzhütte. You can also reach Plattig by a more picturesque path that meanders off at the junction between the two roads (the northern route across the Black Forest signposted with cross-

country skis) and subsequently becomes a road leading directly into Plattig (hotels).

Plattig to Mummelsee   R

13 km (8 miles), 4¼ hours, change in elevation 400 m (1,310 ft)

There are no further problems of orientation from here until the end of the itinerary since the Red Deer trail runs parallel to the Baden-Baden to Freudenstadt road known as the Black Forest autobahn.

From Plattig you proceed to Sand (hotel-restaurant; skilifts) along the cart track running below the road (Nature Trail: 2 km [1¼ miles]). At Sand you rejoin the European Footpath E 1 and the Westweg and follow the signposts for these rather

Above: the northern valley slopes are often too steep to be farmed, but where they open up, scattered remains of the ancient forest can be seen amid the green and rolling countryside.

Left: the signs indicating the Red Deer Trail.

On pages 74 and 75: a panoramic view of the Talsperre artificial lake surrounded by the dark and sometimes impenetrable forest, faithful to its awesome name.

than those of the Red Deer. From Sand keep to the left-hand side of the road passing the Kurhaus Hundseck and the Kurhaus Unterstmatt. Now the most interesting part of this stage begins. The itinerary, in fact, strays some distance from the road through lovely woodland and leads, by a steep ascent, to the panoramic summit of the Hörnisgrinde (1,164 m/3,818 ft), the highpoint of the entire trek. Then there is a short, steep descent to the Mummelsee (1,029 m/3,375 ft; hotel).

Mummelsee to Hotel Schliffkopf   R

24 km (15 miles), 8 hours, change in elevation 50 m (164 ft)

From Mummelsee to Ruhestein the itinerary runs along the left side of the road then takes a broad route up to the Seekopf (1,054 m/3,457 ft; fine view of the Wildsee below). From Ruhestein it runs on the right side and finally climbs gradually to the Hotel Schliffkopf.

Hotel Schliffkopf to Kniebis   R

13 km (8 miles), 4½ hours, change in elevation 100 m (320 ft)

Continue following the Westweg to the right of the road, passing in turn the peaks of the Schurkopf (974 m/3,195 ft), the Plankopf (938 m/3,077 ft) and the Sandkopf (954 m/3,129 ft), and reaching first the Hotel Zuflucht and then the Alexanderschanze. After that the Westweg branches off to the south and you turn left on a path which shortly comes up to cross the road. Soon this brings you to the small town of Kniebis (hotels, guest houses, bed and breakfast).

Kniebis to Freudenstadt   R

12 km (7½ miles), 4 hours, change in elevation 200 m/640 ft

Follow the main road of the town to the open-air swimming pool where the itinerary, again marked with the blue sign, turns right. Having crossed the road, the trail continues on its right through the forest and descends to Freudenstadt where the long circular trek comes to an end.

TOUR DU MONT BLANC

In the Western Alps, over the roof of Europe

Useful addresses: Società delle Guide di Courmayeur, Piazza Henry, Courmayeur, tel. (0)165/842064 (Italy): Syndicat National des Guides de Montagne, 74.4000 Chamonix BP 5, tel. 50.53.10.43 (France). FFRP-CNSGR, Délégation de la Haute Savoie, BP 31 Evian Les Bains Cedex, tel. 50.75.35.87 (France).
Maps: Carte de France, 1:50,000, pp Chamonix-Mont Blanc; St Gervais-Les-Bains; Bourg-St Maurice. Carte Nationale de la Suisse, 1:50,000, Blat feuille 282, Martigny. Carta Turistica Kompass, 1:50,000, Mont Blanc, no. 85.
Bibliography: A. Harper, *Tour of Mont Blanc*, Cicerone Press. Tour du Mont Blanc, topoguide des sentiers de grande randonnée, FFRP, 1986.

The massif of Mont Blanc is a forest of rugged and dangerous peaks welded together in a vast kingdom of ice. And to air passengers on flights between Paris and Milan this mountain group looks like a gigantic iceberg stretching up into the clouds from the encircling green valleys below. Indeed, the dimensions of Mont Blanc, the highest peak in the Alps, are impressive; the massif is 60 km (37 miles) from north to south and between 8 and 15 km (5 and 9¼ miles) in breadth; and this powerful bulwark of rock and ice, shared by France, Italy and Switzerland, is surrounded by a series of wide, deep valleys – the so-called "Seven Valleys" – which cut into its slopes and form a perimeter of about 150 km (93 miles).

The most important of these are: on the Italian side (south-east), the valleys formed by the two branches of the Dora (Val Veni and Italian Val Ferret); and on the French side (north-west), the upper valley of the Arve (the Chamonix Valley). To the west and east the boundaries are marked respectively by the valleys of the rivers Bon Nant (Val Montjoie) and Drance (Swiss Val Ferret).

The interior of the Mont Blanc massif displays a great variety of landscapes. The highest section consists of a line of rounded peaks, Mont Blanc itself, Mont Maudit and Mont Blanc du Tacul, and contains the largest glaciers of the range. They are surrounded by a number of other peaks which, although lower, are even more complex in shape (jagged crests, spires and towers), great walls of red granite which loom up from the valleys beneath to a height of 3,000 m

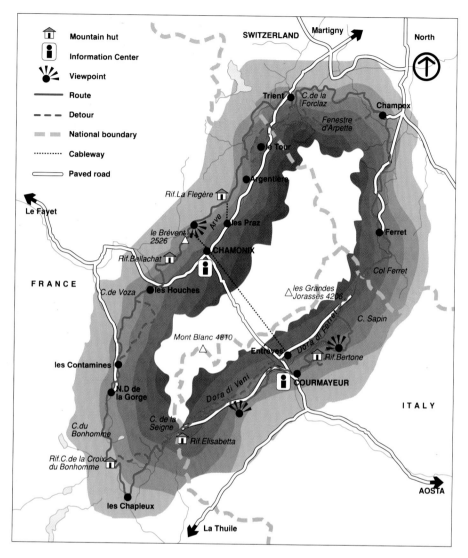

Distance: Itinerary, divided into ten stages.

Departure and arrival points: This is a loop trail linking the valleys of Mont Blanc and can be started at various places: in France from Les Houches, in Italy from Courmayeur and in Switzerland from Champex. Chamonix and Courmayeur are linked by the Mont Blanc tunnel, Chamonix and Champex by the road through Martigny.

Where to stay: All stops at campsites, hostels, and mountain huts (known as *rifugio, refuge, gîte d'étape, dortoir* etc.) offer stocking-up possibilities except at Rifugio Elisabetta in Val Veni.

Recommended hotels: Les Contamines-Montjoie (stage 1); Les Chapieux (stage 2); Courmayeur (stage 4); Ferret (stage 5); Champex (stage 6); Montroc (stage 8); at Forclaz you can spend the night at the hotel on the pass (stage 7) and at La Flégère at the cableway hotel (stage 9).

Signposting: In France and Italy two lines in red and white; in Switzerland a white/red/white flag on mountain routes, yellow diamonds on lower paths.

When to go: In summer, from June to early September.

Difficulty: H. All paths are perfectly negotiable and signposted. Some stages are long and require suitable training but there are numerous places along the way where you can stop if you need. Moreover you can always get back quickly to villages in the valley by road or cablecar.

Equipment: High altitude.

(9,850 ft). Among these are the Aiguille Noire, Aiguille Blanche, Dent du Géant, Grandes Jorasses and Aiguille Verte.

Yet the Tour du Mont Blanc also enables walkers to see some of the longest glaciers in the Alps (there are 70 of them), with views almost rivalling those of the Himalayas. Despite their inevitable shrinking in recent decades, their icy tongues still probe the valley floors, as for example in the case of the glaciers of the Brenva and Miage tributaries of Val Veni, and the glaciers of the Argentière and the Bosson, the white reflections of which create a dazzling colour contrast to the green of the conifer woods. And it is here, on the French side, that the longest glaciers of all, Himalayan in type, are to be found, the record going to the Mer de Glace, a river of ice formed from the confluence of several glaciers and sweeping down 15 km (9¼ miles) to the brink of the Arve Valley.

The vegetation mantling the mountainsides is typically alpine, distributed on the basis of altitude, starting with the broadleaved woods at the valley bottom (ash, hazel, birch), progressing through the belt of conifers and meadows and culminating in the islands of arctic plants springing from the heart of the glaciers.

Mont Blanc in history

The Tour du Mont Blanc for the most part extends along the bottom of the valleys which surround the massif and which link the main towns in the region. Because it crosses from France into Italy and Switzerland, the local styles of building and architecture are very varied, as well as the people themselves.

With the possible exception of the Swiss sector alone, where traditional farming and pastoral activities are most pronounced, there is a common denominator: the growing impact of summer and winter tourism. Even a superficial inspection of the map will show that Mont Blanc appears like a giant surrounded on all sides by roads which snake up to the top of the valleys on its sides and often extend as far as the high alpine pastures; and the massif seems to be under siege from a thick web of cablecars, rack and pinion railways, skilifts, chairlifts and the like, which carry tourists up to viewpoints, up the sides of glaciers and even to the very tops of the mountains themselves. Examples include the train which climbs

THE ALPINE GLACIERS

Glaciers are one of the most typical features of the alpine environment, and their presence heightens the interest and spectacular appeal of any trip through the Western and Central Alps.

A glacier is a mass of slowly and continuously moving ice which originates as a result of the accumulation and gradual transformation of snow. Glaciers therefore occur above the permanent snow line where precipitation is always in the form of snow and this snow remains on the ground even in the warmer months.

There are two principal sections of a glacier: the catchment basin and the ablation basin. The catchment basin is generally a bowl or plateau enclosed by the walls of a mountain where snow accumulates. It is here that the blanket of snow, continuously growing as a result of fresh falls, is transformed little by little into ice. The ablation basin is the continuation of the glacier beneath the permanent snow line. The layers of ice, in fact, through the effect of gravity, slide down below the catchment basin to form an ice tongue. The thermal energy of the sun melts the surface snow and in summer the tongue resembles a mass of greenish or black ice, often covered with detritus of all sorts.

The face of a glacier undergoes various changes: it advances downwards or upwards according to the amount of snowfall and the extent the temperature falls in summer. Expansion and contraction of the ice tongues are the result of the climatic cycle of a series of years. Today glaciers are by and large in a phase of retreat and occupy areas much smaller than in the nineteenth century. Some have formed from the catchment basin from which the downhill tongue branched off. These, the longest, are known as valley glaciers. The record length is that of the Aletsch glacier, in Switzerland's Jungfrau group, which is 25 km (15½ miles) long and which is moving down hill at the speed of half a meter a day.

THE *BISSES*

The "*bisses*," as they are called in the Valais, are irrigation canals which trap the water deriving from glaciers and carry it down to the cultivated fields of the valley below. The oldest date back to the twelfth and thirteenth centuries and were made by prisoners engaged in forced labour, often digging them from the bare rock or scooping them out of tree trunks. Historical research shows that there were 207 *bisses* between Belwald and Champex over a distance of 2,000 km (1,250 miles). Indispensable to the farm economy of the Rhône Valley in periods of dry weather, the ancient irrigation canal network is regarded as worthy of preservation.

On pages 80 and 81: an impressive view of the Mont Blanc group.
Below: the valley of the Arve with Les Houches and the Col de Voza.

from St Gervais up to 2,372 m (7,780 ft) on the Nid d'Aigle, the railway from Chamonix which serves the Hotel de Montenvers overlooking the Mer de Glace, and the spectacular "Glacier Railway," the longest and highest in Europe, which links Courmayeur to Chamonix by way of the Helbronner and the Aiguille du Midi (3,842 m/12,600 ft).

Not even the insides of Mont Blanc have been spared, with a road tunnel of 7 km (4½ miles) running through the middle of the mountain.

Development on such a scale has understandably worried a large section of public opinion and this has resulted in the drawing up of plans to create a Mont Blanc International Park for the future.

However, in the meantime it is difficult for anyone attempting the Tour du Mont Blanc to avoid civilization, given the number of roads, villages, tourist resorts and even cablecar pylons the route encounters. Some of the stages, on the other hand, are through meadows where the only sound is that of the bells of the grazing cows; and there are spots where the ancient thoroughfares, once trodden by pilgrims,

shepherds and soldiers momentarily take you back into times gone by. Finally, the whole journey is naturally to be found in an alpine setting which for sheer grandeur remains unique.

The itinerary

The Tour du Mont Blanc (T.M.B.) consists of a network of paths, all easy to negotiate, covering the lower slopes of the range or the sides of the valleys that encircle it – in France (the Arve, Montjoie and Glacier Valleys), in Italy (Val Veni and Val Ferret) and in Switzerland (Val Ferret, Val de Champex and Val de Trient). It is about 150 km (93 miles) in length and divided into ten stages which take in breathtaking views from the most famous spots.

The possibility of using road access, chairlifts, cablecars etc. makes it easy to reduce or extend the itinerary and take in some of the alternative viewpoints as wished.

The total upward change in elevation is about 7,670 m (25,150 ft).

Above: a bisse, *photographed on the Col de la Forclaz.*

Below: the French Alpine Club refuge near the Col de la Croix du Bonhomme.

Les Houches to Les Contamines R

5¼ hours, change in elevation 800 m (2,625 ft) uphill, 650 m (2,130 ft) downhill

The itinerary begins at the Bellevue cablecar station at Les Houches (1,003 m/3,290 ft), the village at the mouth of the Chamonix Valley, about 4 km (2½ miles) from the main town.

The first stage is to the Col de Voza (1,653 m/5,422 ft) and involves about two hours' walking, first along the road and then up a path through the woods. At Col de Voza you are on a ridge dividing the Arve Valley, behind you, and the lateral valley of Montjoie. There are various places for shopping and refreshments, a skilift and the station of the Mont Blanc Tramway from St Gervais to the Nid d'Aigle. If you do not fancy the climb, take the Bellevue cablecar (1,790 m/5,871 ft) and then come down to Col de Voza by foot alongside the railway track.

From the pass you descend the south slope through a series of meadows to the village of Le Crozat (1,410 m/4,625 ft); a turning to the left leads round the head of the valley, past the bridge crossing the river derived from the Bionnassay glacier above, and then right along the edge of the opposite side of the valley, bringing you to Le Champel (1,200 m/3,936 ft). All that remains is to climb the Montjoie Valley, first by way of the path up the hillside and then by the road leading to Les Contamines (1,161m/3,808 ft), the last major summer and winter resort in the valley (3½–5 ½ hours; 21 hotels; Pontet camping site which also sleeps 30 in huts, tel. 50.47.04.04 [France]).

Les Contamines to Les Chapieux H

7½ hours, change in elevation 1,325 m (4,345 ft) uphill, 930 m (3,050 ft) downhill

This stage takes you up the entire Val Montjoie, once the busiest part of the Mont Blanc massif because of the Roman road from Gaul which ran through it, linking the valley of the Arve with Tarantasia and the Val d'Aosta. This is now a narrow track which extends for some 20 km (12½ miles) below the western slope of Mont Blanc, beginning at La Fayet and ending at the Col du Bonhomme. From Les Contamines, first by road and then along a footpath to its left, you reach the sanctuary of Notre Dame de la Gorge (1,400 m/4,592 ft). Here the old Roman road,

ON THE SUMMIT OF MONT BLANC

Climbing Mont Blanc by the normal routes presents no technical difficulties for those with some training and familiarity with mountain and rock climbing. It could therefore provide an excellent way of rounding off the itinerary, provided you are equipped with ice-axes and crampons and can engage the assistance of a guide.

The easiest ascents lie on the French side and are those of the Bossons glacier and the Dôme de Gouter. The former is much longer because, from the Grands Mulets mountain hut (3,051 m/10,007 ft), where you spend the night, to the summit, you are faced with a change in elevation of some 1,755 m (5,756 ft), taking six hours. The second route, which is the one to be followed in the Tour du Mont Blanc, is more popular. The Les Houches cableway and the Mont Blanc tramway take you conveniently up to the Nid d'Aigle (2,372 m/7,780 ft). From here you start off on foot towards the Aiguille de Gouter mountain hut (3,817 m/12,520 ft; 100 beds; tel. 50.54.40.93 [France]). The most dangerous stretch is across a channel subject to falling stones (fixed safety rope), followed by a climb up a steep rock wall, with metal steps and footholds.

The next day a mere 990 m (3,247 ft) change in elevation ensures an easy, scenic climb to the top of Mont Blanc by way of the Dôme de Gouter and the Refuge Vallot (3–4 hours).

On the Italian side the normal route is along the Miage and Dôme glaciers. The departure point is the Rifugio Gonella (3,071 m/10,073 ft; 4 hours from the Combal lake; stage 4 of itinerary), longer and more strenuous than from the French side (1,735 m/5,691 ft from the hut to the summit).

Opposite: on the descent towards Les Houches, you cross the Arve valley dominated by the Mont Blanc group.

Above: the sanctuary of Notre Dame de la Gorge in the Montjoie valley.

Below: the massif of Mont Blanc, seen from the Helbronner viewpont.

still cobbled, begins and runs along the edge of the deep gorge carved out by the waters (potholes; Contamines-Montjoie Nature Reserve; ¾ hour trip).

Crossing a bridge to the right side of the gorge, you reach the meadows of Nant Borrant (1,457 m/4,479 ft; Chalet-Hotel) and then the Chalet-Hotel of La Balme (1,716 m/5,629 ft). From here there is a view of the col, which you reach by a steep climb through increasingly wild country and broken by the terraces of Plan Jovet (1,940 m/6,363 ft) and Plan des Dames (2,043 m/6,701 ft). From the Col du Bonhomme (2,329 m/7,639 ft) you continue the climb to the left up a stony hillside path which in 50 minutes brings you to the Col de la Croix du Bonhomme (2,483 m/8,144 ft; 4¾–5½ hours; just below the pass is the hut of the French Alpine Club, 30–40 beds).

You now descend to the more isolated valley of Mont Blanc, on the extreme south-western edge of the chain crossed by the Des Glaciers, a tributary of the River Isère. Here there are high meadows, frequented in summer only by shepherds. The most

important village is Les Chapieux, linked by road to Bourg St Maurice, at the foot of the Little St Bernard hill. You reach it in just under one and a half hours by descending a steep path to the pasture of La Raja, then by road (1,554 m/5,097 ft; 1½ hours; Hôtel Gîte de la Terrasse and Auberge de la Nova; camping site).

Detour: From the Col de la Croix du Bonhomme you can avoid the descent to Les Chapieux and proceed directly to Ville des Glaciers (stage 3) over the Col des Fours. The route is through high mountains and poses orientation problems because there are few signs (2¼ hours). Stay overnight at Les Mottets.

Les Chapieux to Rifugio Elisabetta   H

5¼ hours, change in elevation 962 m (3,155 ft) uphill, 316 m (1,036 ft) downhill

Over its first part this is undoubtedly the least varied stage of the trip, but at the same time the tranquillity of the surroundings is compelling. In any event it is the only way of crossing from the French to the Italian side of the massif over the Col de la Seigne, the route of the consular Roman road from Gaul, perhaps the one taken by Hannibal during the second Punic War.

From Les Chapieux you follow the road that climbs the valley past Séloge (1,809 m/5,933 ft; camping site with 48 beds in huts) to the summer pasture of Ville des Glaciers (1,789 m/5,868 ft). Cross the river and continue along the left side of the valley to Les Mottets (1,864 m/6,114 ft; chalet with 60–70 beds; 2 hours). From here, after a series of twists and turns, you reach the Col de la Seigne (2,516 m/8,252 ft; 2 hours), with a marvellous view over the entire southern slope of Mont Blanc and beyond to the distant Aiguille Noire de Peuterey, ample compensation for the effort needed to get here.

From the col you come down into Italy to the Alpe Supérieure de la Lex Blanche and around the foot of the Pyramides Calcaires to the Alpe Inférieure de la Lex Blanche. Close to the glacier of that name dominated by the Aiguille de Trelatète is the mountain hut, Rifugio Elisabetta Soldini, reached also by a road from the bottom of the valley (2,200 m/7,216 ft; 1–5 hours; 60 beds, tel. (0)165/843743 [Italy]).

THE CONQUEST OF MONT BLANC

In a square in Courmayeur there is a bronze statue of Balmat pointing out the summit of Mont Blanc to the famous Geneva scientist Horace-Benedict de Saussure, as if suggesting the ascent route. It was de Saussure who in 1760 promised a prize of three guineas to the first man to the get to the top.

Twenty-six years were to pass, however, before the dream was realized while in the meantime Chamonix developed into a fashionable tourist resort (three hotels and 500 summer homes) thanks to the writings and drawings of M. T. Bourrit, determined to be the first to reach the summit of Mont Blanc. His rival was Gabriel Paccard, a young doctor from Chamonix. The two attempted the climb, first together, then separately, by two different routes – the Montagne de la Côte and the Aiguille de Gouter. But it was Paccard, after examining the Brévent peak through binoculars, who first identified the best route along the Bosson glacier. Paccard made his attempt, on 7 August 1786, accompanied by the crystal prospector Jacques Balmat, and at 18:23 on the same day the two men reached the long-desired goal. Jealous of the achievement, Bourrit initiated a defamatory campaign against Paccard, giving all the credit for the triumphant ascent to Balmat; the king of Sardinia recognized the latter with a money prize and the right to add "of Mont Blanc" to his name, while Paccard was entirely forgotten. A year later de Saussure's moment arrived as well. Balmat had paved the way for him and built two huts for overnight stays. On 3 August 1787, accompanied by his personal servant and seventeen guides with provisions, rung ladders, a bed, a stove and scientific equipment (hygrometers, barometers and thermometers), the scientist from Geneva fulfilled his dream by reaching the summit as the bells of the villages in the valley rang out in celebration.

Above: a young chamois photographed in the Aiguilles Rouges nature reserve.

Below: high in the Alps, the warm light of the setting sun bathes the peaks and slopes.

Rifugio Elisabetta to Courmayeur   R

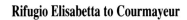

3½ hours, change in elevation 976 m (3,201 ft) downhill

The first of the two Italian stages of the journey is the descent of Val Veni to Courmayeur. The lush green valley was once only occupied by summer pastures but with the opening of a military road used during the World War, these have since developed into small tourist spots. In winter the road is closed and the valley is only accessible to those using skilifts from the Courmayeur region and to cross-country skiing enthusiasts.

From the trekking point of view, therefore, there is nothing in the basic itinerary to point out except for the magnificent scenery and incidental natural features.

A road leads down from the mountain hut to the great moraine of the Miage glacier which closes the valley and forms the Combal lake, now reduced to a swamp. Crossing the bridge over the river, take a short diversion to the left of the road and climb the steep path to the crest of the moraine, to the Miage

pool (2,020 m/6,625 ft; departure point for the mountain hut Rifugio Gonella along the normal road up towards Mont Blanc).

Proceeding along the road, now paved, you reach the Visaille (public transport service to Courmayeur). Cross the Plan Veni meadows, pass the chapel of Notre Dame de la Guérison and continue to Courmayeur (3¼ hours; 80 hotels; overnight stay facilities at the Hotel Funivia di La Palud).

This last stretch is notable for the splendid Brenva glacier which extends almost to the entrance of the Mont Blanc tunnel below the village of Entrèves.

Detour: An extremely interesting scenic route goes along the hillside of the northern slope of the Val Veni, recommended for anyone who wishes to avoid the valley road and enjoy a better view of the entire Mont Blanc group (H).

At the Combal Lake you take a path on the right which leads to the Arp Vieille Superior (2,303 m/7,554 ft) and continues along the hillside, with many ups and downs, to the small lake, Chécrouit (2,165 m/7,102 ft). From here you can make a short

THE GLACIER RAILWAY

This is the longest and highest cable railway in Europe, providing passengers with a spectacular aerial view of the biggest glacier in the Mont Blanc range. From Courmayeur two branches of the line travel in 20 minutes up to the Punta Helbronner (3,452 m/11,322 ft; Rifugio Torino; summer ski facilities). After frontier formalities, the railway enters French territory. The tiny cablecars move along the north wall of the Tour Rondre and then cross the Glacier du Géant and Vallée Blanche to reach the Aiguille du Midi (3,842 m/12,602 ft), which concludes the trip. From here two more lines run down to Chamonix-Mont Blanc. Regarded as one of the marvels of modern engineering, the cableway is unacceptable to the Mountain Wilderness movement which demands the dismantling of the central sector in order to leave Mont Blanc to be climbed by mountaineers alone.

Above: the tongue of the Pré de Bar glacier in the Italian Val Ferret with its perfectly rounded end.

climb to the cablecar station of the Chécrouit which runs straight down to Courmayeur; alternatively make for the Col Chécrouit and then descend again to the Val Veni by the way of the mountain hut and camping site of the Italian Alpine Club (calculate 2½ hours or more for the walk).

Courmayeur to Ferret   H

8 hours, change in elevation 1,320 m (4,329 ft) uphill, 835 m (2,739 ft) downhill

The second Italian stage is through Val Ferret, a long walk of about 15 km (9½ miles) from the village of Entrèves (1,306 m/4,284 ft) to the Col du Gran Ferret (2,543 m/8,341 ft). The broad, level floor of the valley is studded with pastures and modern houses and overlooked, from a height of over 4,000 m (13,120 ft), by the peaks of the Dent du Géant, the Grandes Jorasses and the Aiguille de Triolet. Equally imposing are the glaciers, all suspended except for those of Triolet and Pré de Bar, which extend down to the valley itself.

A road through the valley climbs to the Alpe Pré de Bar but is open to motor traffic only as far as the plain of the Arnuva (1,769 m/5,802 ft; 13 km/8 miles). In winter the road is closed to traffic and the cross-country ski route around the valley is one of the loveliest in the Alps.

From Courmayeur you can reach Val Ferret by public transport or on foot along the path which runs from La Saxe, winds around the right side of the Dora and finally joins up with the road at Planpincieux (1,579 m/5,179 ft; 1½ hours). From here you follow the road to Arnuva and then climb to the Alpe Pré de Bar situated right opposite the glacier of that name, famous for its characteristic face (new hotel with 100 beds; 2,062 m/6,763 ft; 2¾ hours).

From the alp follow the sharp turns through the meadows up to the Col du Gran Ferret (2,537 m/8,321 ft; 1½ hours) which looks down on the Val Ferret in Switzerland, with a path running gently down and finally joining the road to the village of Ferret (1,707 m/5,600 ft; 2 hours; Hotel-Restaurant, tel. 26.411.80 [Switzerland]; 30 beds).

Detour: To avoid the road of the Italian Val Ferret, you can take the following route, which has become an integral part of the Tour du Mont Blanc: Courmayeur – Villair – Le Pré (Rifugio Bertone hut, 1,991

m/6,530 ft) – Montagne de la Saxe – Col Sapin – Alpe de Sécheron – Malatra – La Vachey. This involves a change in elevation of more than 1,000 m (3,200 ft) upward and about six hours' walking, but it includes the broadest panorama of mountain scenery on the Italian side. It can be treated as an additional stage or linked with the previous one by staying overnight at Rifugio Bertone instead of the hotel in Courmayeur (60 beds, tel. (0)165/844612 [Italy]).

Ferret to Champex R

4½ hours, change in elevation 415 m (1,361 ft) uphill, 650 m (2,132 ft) downhill

This is a very short stage which can also be done entirely by bus; but only by walking can you really appreciate the special charm of this valley, so different from the Italian side. The summer and winter tourist resorts (Praz de Fort and Champex) are busy

Below: shepherds' cottages built on the summer pastures; the architectural style of those below is particular to the Italian Val Ferret.

Above: the Mont Blanc group, seen from the Aiguilles Rouges nature reserve; a magnificent spectacle unaffected either by time or human encroachment.

all year round, yet the pastoral landscape remains unspoiled, with its characteristic barns, chapels, fountains and drinking troughs. Strawberries are grown here and the green woods, formerly a timber reserve for the Great St Bernard Hospice (reached via the Col de la Fenêtre) make a vivid contrast to the glaciers and red granite walls of the Argentière massif.

Proceed along the road from Ferret to La Fouly and then, crossing a bridge over the Drance de Ferret, take the path through the woods on the left side of the valley, across the ancient moraine of the Seleina glacier which descends from the Aiguille d'Argentière, arriving first at Praz de Fort (hotel and restaurant) and then Issert (1,056 m/3,464 ft; 2½ hours). Here the path leads away from the valley floor and winds through dense conifer woods to reach the large tourist resort of Champex (1,472 m/4,828 ft; 2 hours; French Alpine Club chalet, 15 beds, tel. 26.411.61; Chalet le Belvedere, 15 beds, tel.

26.411.14; Chalet en Plein Air, 60 beds, tel.
36.423.50; camping; tourist information office, tel.
36.411.227 [all Swiss tel. no.s]).

Champex Lac to Col de la Forclaz   H

5½ hours, change in elevation 700 m (2,296 ft)
uphill, 690 m (2,263 ft) downhill

From Champex, situated above the Val Ferret with
its small lake, the route continues through a delightful area of meadows, fields and woods, with distant
glimpses of the most northerly peaks of the range and
views over the vineyards and orchards of the Martigny plain. The standard route goes through Champex de Haut, Champex d'en Bas and Plan d'Eau and
leads to the Bovine summer pasture, a famous viewpoint over a wide bend of the Rhine, the Bernese
Alps and the central Valais (4 hours).

    From Bovine you climb about 100 m (100 yards) up
a small hill and then begin the descent to the La Giète

Below: rural architecture in the Swiss Val Ferret.

On pages 96 and 97: the Mont Blanc group with, in the background, the crests of the Aiguille Noire and the Aiguille Blanche de Peuterey, and the Brenva glacier.

Below: the Brouillard glacier, dominated by the massive peak of Mont Blanc, seen from the Val Veni.

chalet and the Col de la Forclaz (1,527 m/5,008 ft; road from Martiny to Chamonix; bus service; chairlift to the Arpille viewpoint; 1½ hours; Hôtel du Col and chalet, 75 beds, tel. 26.226.88 [Switzerland]). **Detour:** You can also reach the col by a more strenuous route which, shortly after Champex, climbs the Val d'Arpette, crosses the Fenêtre Arpette (2,665 m/8,741 ft) and then leads down to the Alpe Vesevei and the Chalet du Glacier. The walk is chiefly interesting for the outflow of the Trient glacier, the full grandeur of which can be admired as it descends to the col.

Col de la Forclaz to Montroc   H

5½ hours, change in elevation 730 m (2,394 ft)
uphill, 860 m (2,821 ft) downhill

This stage marks the end of the journey across the
northern slopes of the Mont Blanc range in Switzerland; from the Trient valley the route returns to
France, via the Col de Balme to the Arve valley.

From the Col de la Forclaz, on the other side of the
road, a path leads to Prise du Bisse (1,592 m/5,222 ft;
¾ hour; Peuty hostel, 50 beds, tel. 26.223.97.50
[Switzerland]; camping site). Cross the stream flowing from the Trient glacier and climb to the pasture of
Les Grands; then there is a short descent to the Alpe
Remonteise (2,078 m/6,816 ft; 1½ hours).

Continuing along the hillside, it is a gentle climb to
the Alpe d'Herbagères (2,033 m/6,668 ft) and then
comes the final stony slope up to the Col de Balme
(2,204 m/7,229 ft; 1½ hours; chalet-hotel in Swiss
territory close to the frontier).

From the col there is an extraordinary view over
the whole valley of the Arve, including Chamonix
and the north face of Mont Blanc.

The path comes down through meadows to the
village of Le Tour and you reach Montroc by walking
along the side of the road (1,389 m/4,556 ft; 1½
hours; railway station on the Chamonix–Martigny
line; hotels; Le Moulin hostel at Aux Frasserands, 44
beds, tel. 50.54.05.37 [France]). You can also come
down by the cablecar which links the Col de Balme
with Le Tour in two stages.

Montroc to La Flégère   H

4½ hours, change in elevation 785 m (2,575 ft)
uphill, 350 m (1,148 ft) downhill

The last two stages are on the right side of the
Chamonix valley, along the slopes of the Aiguilles
Rouges and the Montagne de la Flégère up to the top
of the Brevent. It offers a real balcony view of Mont
Blanc and its glaciers – a spectacular climax to the
itinerary.

From Montroc leave the road near the station, pass
the Bellevue hotel and climb through the woods as
far as the junction with the Chamonix–Martigny
road at Tré le Champ (1,417 m/4,648 ft; hostel Gîte
d'Etapes La Boerne; ½ hour).

Cross the road and prepare for the long, steep

THE OLD ROADS

The oldest thoroughfare with remains
of the original cobbles which can still
partly be walked over is the path which
climbed from the Arve valley up the
Montjoie valley to the Col du Bonhomme at the southernmost tip of the
range. From here ran the consular road
from Gaul which divided at Les Chapieux; one branch led north over the Col
de la Seigne and into the Val d'Aosta,
the other continued south and joined up
with the roads of the Little St Bernard
and of Mont Cenis. In the second half of
the seventeenth century the Waldensès
chose this road for their "glorious re-
entry" to the Valle Pellice after three
years in the Protestant Swiss cantons.
This was an epic journey reminiscent of
the exodus of the Jews under Moses, in
which 2,000 Waldenses, equipped and
armed, fled the troops of Victor
Amadeus II and, according to the an-
nals, ". . . climbed one of the most difficult passes of the mountain known as
the Bel-Homme amid snow and continuous rain . . . where thirty men managed to halt an entire army."

At that time the two sides of Mont
Blanc were already politically united
under the Savoyard dynasty and this
had led to even closer links between the
inhabitants of Savoy and the Val
d'Aosta. From Chamonix, according to
contemporary reports, people crossed
the Colle del Gigante to attend Mass in
the parish of Courmayeur and many
Savoyard mountain dwellers were
forced to migrate seasonally to the Val
d'Aosta where they were welcomed for
their cheese-making skills. The road
they used was the most direct one from
the Argentière glacier, from the Col du
Dolent and the Val Ferret. The crossing
of such high passes was possible because
of the retreat of the glaciers during a
period when the climate was very good.
At the end of the eighteenth century the
glaciers began to advance again, block-
ing not only the passes but also threatening the villages themselves.

climb which also involves an ascent to the rocky crag of the Aiguillette d'Argentière (two good tracks with steps and railings) at a height of 2,132 m (6,993 ft). Ignore the branch on the right that leads to Lac Blanc, and continue left, gradually coming down to the chalet of Chéserys (2¾ hours); from here there is a long trek across the slopes of the Aiguilles Rouges above the wooded nature reserve to the cablecar station of La Flégère (1,875 m/6,150 ft; 1¼ hours; refuge with 100 beds, tel. 50.53.06.13 [France]; cablecar down to Chamonix-Le Praz).

La Flégère to Les Houches

5½ hours, change in elevation 685 m (2,247 ft) uphill, 1,521 m (4,990 ft) downhill

From Flégère continue along the hillside, past the ruins of the Chalet de Charlanon and up to Plan Praz, the intermediate station on the Chamonix–Le Brévent cableway (2,000 m/6,550 ft; 1 hour).

The presence of the cable railway does not detract from the charm of the Brévent, which was climbed several times in the eighteenth century by those attempting the first ascent of Mont Blanc and working out the best route. Le Brévent is in fact a splendid viewpoint: looming over everything is the snow-capped peak of Mont Blanc and the Bossons glacier; to the left are Mont Maudit, Mont Blanc du Tacul, the Aiguille du Midi and the Aiguille du Chamonix; and in the distance, beyond the Mer de Glace, the Aiguille Verte and the Drus. If you do not want to take the cablecar, you can walk up to the Col de Brévent along the wide tracks of the ski pistes and reach the top by way of the northern slope which is often still snow covered in early summer (2,524 m/8,278 ft; 2 hours).

All that now remains is the long descent to the valley. The path comes down along the north side towards the Brévent lake which can be seen below, then it crosses a small hill and returns to the ridge; further down it bends to the left and the steep, winding descent continues (Gîte d'Etapes Bellachat hostel, 30 beds; ¾ hour) through the wood to the Merlet plateau (1,480 m/4,854 ft; zoo with entrance fee) linked to Les Houches by road. Follow this for 300 m (300 yards), then take the path leading to the bottom of the valley near the station of Les Houches after passing the statue of *Le Christ Roi* (1¾ hours).

GIANTS' TRAIL

In the Val d'Aosta, at the foot of Monte Rosa, the Matterhorn and Mont Blanc

The *Alta Via dei Giganti* takes in the "Giants" Mont Blanc (4,810 m/15,777 ft), Gran Combin (4,314 m/14,150 ft), Matterhorn (4,478 m/14,688 ft) and Monte Rosa (15,200 ft), whose peaks and glaciers form the western and northern boundaries of the Val d'Aosta.

At their feet a series of deeply grooved valleys extend from north to south and open out into the main valleys below. Their streams are all left-hand tributaries of the Dora Baltea, with its source in the slopes of Mont Blanc, the confluence point of the Dora di Ferret and Dora di Veni.

The first valley at the eastern entrance to the Val d'Aosta is the Gressoney, enclosed by the peaks Castor (4,226 m/13,861 ft) and Lyskamm (4,527 m/14,848 ft), with the great Lys glacier.

Next comes the Val d'Ayas with the Evançon river and the Verra glaciers dominated by the Breithorn, the Pollux and the Castor.

Further west are the Valsaveranche, where the Rosa group merges with that of the Matterhorn. On the Swiss–Italian border, the Matterhorn itself (Fr. Mont Cervin, Ital. Monte Cervino), with its elegant and unmistakable pyramidal shape, is arguably the most recognizable mountain in the world.

Forming part of the Matterhorn group is the short stretch of the St Barthélemy valley and the Valpelline, with a secondary branch, the Ollomont valley, extending to the foothills of the Gran Combin. This leads to the Great St Bernard valley, the only

Useful addresses: Ufficio Informazioni Turistiche, Piazza Chanoux 8, Aosta, tel. (0)165/35655; Azienda di Promozione Turistica *at* Gressoney La Trinité, tel. (0)125/366143, Breuil/Cervinia, tel. (0)166/949136, Courmayeur (0)165/842060; Servizio Meterologico (weather report), St Christophe, Strada Nazionale, tel. (0)165/44113.
Maps: Kompass 1:50,000, pp 85 (Mont Blanc/Monte Bianco) and 87 (Breuil/Cervinia-Zermatt); Istituto Geografico Centrale, 1:50,000, pp 4 and 5.
Bibliography: *Valle d'Aosta, le Alte Vie*, four-language pamphlet available at tourist offices above.

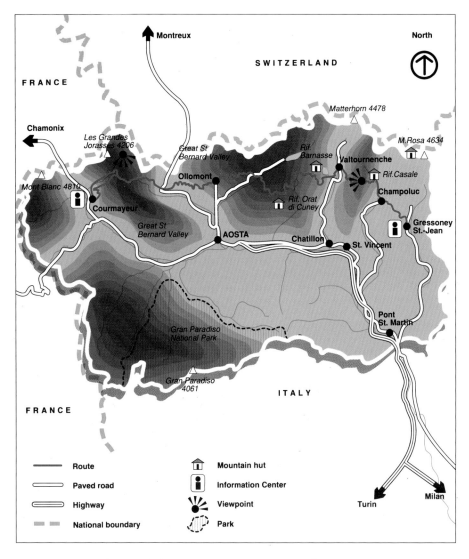

Distance: 120 km (75 miles), divided into eight stages.

Departure point: Gressoney St Jean (1,385 m/4,543 ft). On the Turin–Aosta autostrada exit at Pont St Martin and then take the Val di Gressoney road (33 km/20 miles); by rail to Pont St Martin station on Turin–Aosta–Morgex line and by bus (bus company SAVDA, tel. (0)165/361244).

Arrival point: Courmayeur (1,224 m/4,014 ft); 30 km (18 miles) from Aosta.

Where to stay: The Giants' Trail runs through a number of villages where you can stay the night and buy provisions in general stores. Overnight hotel stays at St Jacques (Val d'Ayas), Cheneil (Valtournanche), Dzovenno and Ollomont (Valpelline), Cuchepache (hamlet of Bosses, Great St Bernard valley); overnight stays in refuges only possible at Rifugio Barmasse on Lake Cignana (stage 3) and Rifugio Cuney near the Cuney sanctuary (stage 4), but take your own provisions. In Val d'Aosta free camping is prohibited.

Signposting: Yellow triangles and direction indicators marked with number 1.

Difficulty: H. The Giants' Trail is exclusively on marked paths but in its central sector it crosses wild and isolated zones far from built-up areas. Adequate training is needed to cope with changes in elevation. However, it is always possible to reach a village in the valley, should you need to.

When to go: July–August.

Equipment: High altitude.

valley on this side of the Val d'Aosta with a road carrying international traffic which, through the St Bernard pass, travels between Italy and Switzerland.

Our brief overview ends at Mont Blanc, looming above the broad, lush Val Ferret with its eastern section of the Grandes Jorasses at Mont Dolent, marking the boundary of the Pennine Alps and the Graian Alps.

In its entirety this is one of the most impressive high mountain environments of the Alpine chain, shaped to a great extent by the enormous glaciers which in the Quaternary flowed into the Aosta valley's river of ice. Today they have all retreated to high altitudes, leaving behind spectacular push moraine along which the paths are often found, cirques worn out in the rock and sometimes occupied by picturesque pools, characteristic U-shaped valleys and, below, on the rim of Val d'Aosta, high terraces carved out in the rock by the courses of rivers.

The trees that grow along this high mountain route consist primarily of conifers, which grow at a height of almost 2,000 m (6,300 ft), in association with arolla pine (*Pinus cembra*) and larch (*Larix decidua*). Higher still is the zone of alpine meadows where one of the plants to be found is the alpine yarrow (*Achillea moschata*), gathered by the valley inhabitants to make the most well-known liqueur in the Aosta region, genepi.

The people of the valleys

The Giants' Trail links the valleys on the left side of the Val d'Aosta in the shelter of the mountain peaks and for the most part following age-old tracks which the valley folk have used over the centuries for a variety of purposes: trade, hunting and the movement of livestock to new pastures.

The people who live here and the way of life are therefore very interesting. Many of the stages in this itinerary culminate in a sleepy village where, in spite of tourist development, local styles of architecture have been preserved. In the valleys of the Lys and Ayas, because the local inhabitants came originally from the Valais, the dominant building material is wood, used in the traditional *rascard* or *stadel* structure. The original irrigation canals which caught the melting glacier water and carried it down to the

---

THE ALPINE FAUNA

It is interesting to note how, like the flowers, the local animals are well adapted, both physically and physiologically, to the mountain environment. The commonest examples of adaptation are: increased fur and plumage to protect against the cold; migrations from one altitude to another; hibernation among mammals; colour modifications of fur and plumage – white in winter (albinism) and dark in summer to provide camouflage and self-defense – with a tendency towards melanism in certain animals (salamander, viper, etc.) wherever dark colours provide protection against ultraviolet rays and against the cold by facilitating the absorption of heat. One of the animals you are most likely to encounter during an alpine trek, having recently increased immeasurably in numbers because of a protection policy, is the marmot.

The marmot is a hibernating animal with a distribution range that includes, in addition to Europe, Asia and North America. The alpine marmot (*Marmota marmota*) lives at heights from 1,300 m (4,265 ft) to 1,500 m (4,920 ft), preferably in areas with plenty of grass. At a glance it is hard to distinguish the creature because it blends so well with the rocks beneath which it digs its burrow. But the unmistakable alarm whistle, which it uses as an acoustic system of communication, enables you to identify the whereabouts of this attractive rodent. In such circumstances it adopts the characteristic upright position, rising up on its hind feet. The marmot does not live on its own but in colonies made up of different families. Each family possesses a territory of 14,000–20,000 m² (150,000–215,000 sq. ft) and consists of an adult male, one or more adult females, the newborn and a variable number of young marmots. Even a brief halt in a walk may give you a chance to see the young and baby marmots indulging in the games they play for much of the time during summer.

THE GERMAN CANTON

Until quite recently the upper Val d'Ayas was so named because it was inhabited by colonies of Valdesi, nowadays known by the generic name of Waldenses.

These are people speaking the Tisch language who settled at the heads of the southern valleys of Monte Rosa during the Middle Ages on the orders of the Waldensian landed proprietors. Their task was to garrison the passes which were then easily accessible.

Thanks to more favourable climatic conditions, the glaciers were then shorter than they are today and the highest of them, forming a bridge between one valley and another, could even be crossed without difficulty, either for military or commercial reasons.

The descendants of the Tisch still live in the Lys and Ayas valleys, forming German-speaking islands in a region where the *valdostano* dialect prevails. Typical features of their architecture are the *rascards* and *stadels*, barns and homes built with squared-off tree trunks which are angled together with a double joint. The floor is raised from the ground supported by mushroom-shaped pillars on a stone base. This system protected the building from damp and from rodents. In many buildings the space below the pillars consisted of a room in stone used as either a cattle shed or living quarters, with the traditional wooden casing resting on the pillars over it.

Rarer, and restricted to the Gressoney valley, are houses with large balconies covered in trellises once used for drying hay.

On pages 102 and 103: the south face of the Matterhorn.

Right: the Dora di Ferret on its lively course through the Val Ferret.

drought-prone fields at the bottom of the valley testify to the old farming economy, nowadays replaced by tourism and all its ramifications.

A wealth of fields and meadows fostered the traditional activity of livestock rearing and locally this still flourishes, based on the seasonal movement of animals from their winter quarters in the villages down below to the summer pastures which are owned by farming communes or cooperatives. This entails the creation of veritable temporary villages, furnished with the traditional shepherds' cottages and cattle sheds, which are occupied only in July and August. Some of the most typical of these, taking the form of a series of rooms, often partially underground with barrel-vaulted ceilings, are encountered in the final stage of the itinerary. Here it is still possible to watch the various phases of milk production and the manufacture of the famous Valdostana cheese (*fontina*), basic ingredient for several characteristic local dishes (*fonduta* and *polenta concia*, a type of fondue and a cheesy cornmeal dish).

The Giants' Trail shows the trekker the two contrasting faces of the Val d'Aosta: one, that of the elegant, winter sports resorts, with its apartments and skilifts (typified by the Breuil/Cervinia); the other, that of unspoiled stretches of landscape where the only shelter is often no more than an isolated mountain hut.

The itinerary

The route of the Giants' Trail (officially the *Alta Via della Valle d'Aosta No. 1*), planned and opened in 1977, joins together all the lateral valleys on the left side of the Val d'Aosta, bounded by the groups of Monte Rosa, the Matterhorn, the Gran Combin and Mont Blanc.

The main reason for choosing this trip is therefore to see the gigantic peaks of 4,000 m (13,120 ft) and more along each of the eight stages, constituting a total distance of about 120 km (75 miles).

The basic itinerary leads from one valley to another along historic paths and across passes which are easy to negotiate but which at the same time involve marked changes in elevation. It links a number of villages which frequently offer overnight accommodation: St Jacques, Crétaz, Dzovenno, Ollomont, Cuchepache and Courmayeur. The total change

THE CLIMBING OF THE MATTERHORN

After numerous attempts, the Matterhorn was conquered on 14 July 1865 by the English mountaineer Edward Whymper who succeeded in climbing the north-east face (Hörnli ridge), ahead of the Italian party guided by the bersagliere, Carrel, ascending by the more difficult south-west face (Leone ridge). The descent, however, was darkened by tragedy. When one of Whymper's companions slipped, he also dragged to their deaths the three climbers linked to him by rope, and it was only by good fortune that Whymper himself and two others on his rope were saved. On their return court proceedings were opened to determine whether the rope broke accidentally or whether it was deliberately cut. Arguments ensued which filled the front pages of Swiss newspapers and later provided excellent subject matter for a number of romanticized film versions.

Today the Matterhorn is climbed every year by hundreds of mountaineers. The normal route is the one taken by Whymper, on the Swiss side, longer than the Italian but considerably easier. The steepest and most exposed stretch (where the tragedy occurred) is protected by fixed ropes. The Leone ascent is much more arduous and includes grade IV sections, all requiring ladders and fixed ropes. The starting point is the Rifugio Carrel at the Grande Tour (3,830 m/12,562 ft; 5 hours from Breuil/Cervinia). From here a climb of 4–5 hours brings one to the Italian peak (large cross, 4,476 m/14,681 ft) and along a level ridge to the Swiss peak (Matterhorn, 4,478 m/14,688 ft).

Non-expert climbers must be accompanied by a guide (refer to Casa delle Guide di Breuil/Cervinia; adjoining museum full of interesting curiosities associated with the Matterhorn and expeditions outside Europe pioneered by the Guide della Valtournanche).

in elevation uphill is about 8,910 m (29,225 ft).

Several detours from the standard route are included here. They go rather higher, to the heads of valleys and close to the great glaciers. For more expert trekkers these offer attractive alternatives to the first three stages.

Chemonal to St Jacques d'Ayas   H

8½ hours, change in elevation 1,370 m (4,493 ft) uphill, 1,088 m (3,569 ft) downhill

The departure point is Chemonal (1,385 m/4,543 ft) on the road linking Gressoney St Jean to Gressoney la Trinité. The bridle path climbs first to the farmsteads at Alpenzù Grande, then proceeds north-west along the hillside, entering the Pinter valley at the level of the Alpe Loange (lower, middle and upper). From here there is a steep ascent through meadows and detritus to the Colle di Pinter, a deep incision in the mountain of that name (1,777 m/5,828 ft; 4½ hours). Beautiful view of the Ruitor group and Mont Blanc.

There is a descent on the opposite slope of the pass to a shelf (on the left are the two small Pinter lakes) and the path then leads through a narrow rock channel into the Cunéaz valley. You pass the Lavassay mountain chalets, the architectural style of which is similar to that of Gressoney, and the France and Creste ones. Then instead of going down through the wood to Champoluc, you bear right. The path now continues along the hillside on the left side of the Val d'Ayas, passes the lateral valley of Contenery and eventually descends to St Jacques (4 hours). You can spend the night in one of the village hotels or at the Rifugio Casale which is situated on the path before reaching the village (32 beds; tel. (0)125/307668).

St Jacques to Valtournanche   H

5 hours, change in elevation 1,086 m (3,562 ft) uphill, 1,251 m (4,103 ft) downhill

The path begins at the bridge near the church and continues along the hillside by way of the farmsteads Drole and Rovinal, joining the road which climbs the Val de Nana to the Alpe di Nana Alta (2,194 m/7,196 ft).

Continue on the path for the upper and lower Alpe Tournalin, and from the latter climb to the Col di

Nana between the Becca Trecaré and the Bec de Nana (2,775 m/9,102 ft; 3 hours). Formed of characteristic white rocks, the col offers a fine view over the Grandes Murailles and the mountains of the Valais.

Descend to the head of the Chamois valley, leaving on your left path 54 which branches off towards the village of Chamois, linked to the valley below only by cablecar, and cross the broad saddle of the Colle di Croux (path 2; 2,697 m/8,846 ft) into the Alpe Champsec valley and thence to the village of Cheneil (2,105 m/6,904 ft; 2 hours).

Valtournanche is situated lower down but the splendid position of the basin, dominated by the Grand Tournalin, invites an overnight stay at the Albergo Panorama (1,524 m/4,998 ft; 20 beds; tel. (0)166/92019). This hotel also accommodates the L. Carrel school of mountain-climbing.

The summit of the Matterhorn with the Furggen and Hörnli crests (the usual Swiss route).

View of the Monte Rosa chain with the Castor peak and the Rollin hump.

Cheneil to Rifugio Barmasse   H

3½ hours, change in elevation 645 m (2,115 ft) uphill, 581 m (1,905 ft) downhill

This is the shortest stage of the route and can be done at leisure, stopping at the most interesting places, both scenic and archaeological. From Cheneil you descend into the wood at the hamlet of Crétaz (¾ hour), cross the road to the bottom of the valley and take path 13 which leads up to the hamlet of Barmasse (1,493 m/4,897 ft).

Just outside the village you pass underneath an impressive rock, where you should stop to see the remains of rock carvings that date back to the Iron Age, even though they have been much defaced. Now comes a winding climb and then bear left to the houses of Promoron (1,798 m/5,897 ft; pressure water pipe); at the time of the construction of the

THE CUNEY SANCTUARY

The sanctuary of Cuney stands as witness to a bygone age of religious settlement in mountain regions. Founded in 1650 by the Benedictine monks, it is situated at a height of 2,652 m (8,698 ft) near the top of the Freideront valley, a lateral branch of the St Barthélemy valley. In the past it was the destination of pilgrimages.

It is linked with Lignan (1,633 m/ 5,356 ft) by a bridle path – a walk of 3½ hours – and used to be accessible as well to the inhabitants of the Valpelline by way of the Colle de Cuney.

Restored and enlarged in 1869, it consists of a single building with the chapel and several adjacent rooms. The sanctuary was described in the famous *Histoire de la Vallée d'Aoste* by Abbot Henry, parish priest of Valpelline for 44 years, himself an enthusiastic walker and climber who explored the valley. According to the abbot, Cuney means "au cul," namely at the foot of the snow, and local people gave the name "coneia" to several species of yarrow which grew on the shores of the lake near the sanctuary and which were gathered in the summer months for sale to herbalists.

Cignana dam this was the terminus for the 6-km (3¾-mile) service railway from Les Perères. Continue climbing past the Falegnon houses (1,912 m/ 6,271 ft), then leave path 13 which bears left towards the Alpe Cortina and proceed along the left side of the valley to the outskirts of the dam where the Rifugio Barmasse stands on high ground (2,169 m/ 7,114 ft; 2½ hours; 27 beds; tel. (0)165/40996).

Rifugio Barmasse to Santuario di Cuney　　E

8 hours, change in elevation 1,500 m (4,920 ft) uphill, 950 m (3,116 ft) downhill

Crossing the head of the St Barthélemy valley, one of the wildest and most unspoiled in the Val d'Aosta, you plunge into a harsh, solitary landscape. This is a long and complicated stage, with an alternation of ascents and descents.

THE GRAN PARADISO NATIONAL PARK

With an area of 70,000 hectares (173,000 acres), the Gran Paradiso National Park lies in the regions of Piedmont and the Val d'Aosta. It is made up of five main valleys: Orco and Soana, on the Piedmontese side, Cogne, Valsavaranche and Rhêmes on the Aosta side. The two sides are separated by a great mountain chain dominated by the peak of Gran Paradiso (4,061 m/13,320 ft), the highest mountain in the park and the only one of over 4,000 m (13,120 ft) to be found entirely in Italian territory.

Visitor center and access: The administration office is in Turin and should be consulted for all information concerning free and guided visits (Via della Rocca, 47). On the spot you can contact the local Aziende di Turismo e Pro Loco (Cogne, Piazza Chanoux, tel. (0)165/74040; Valsavaranche, Pro Loco di Degioz (0)165/95703; Val di Rhêmes, Pro Loco di Notre Dame (0)165/96144).

The park contains a number of houses, kiosks, and service points for the rangers which are at the public's disposal only in cases of emergency. Free camping is prohibited inside the park so you can only spend the night in the alpine refuges. The only official campgrounds are at Valnontey, Pont Valsavaranche, St George and Notre Dame in the Val de Rhêmes.

Itineraries: These are many and varied. For a short visit you must, above all, choose the Cogne valley leading to the Valnontey valley, perhaps the best known and most fascinating part of the whole park. Here, among other things, is the Paradisia Alpine Botanical Garden, created by the park authorities in 1965 over an area of 10,000 m^2 (107,650 sq. ft; open to the public every day from 15 June to 15 September; entrance fee; for parties of more than 15 people advance bookings are taken at the administrative offices, tel. (0)165/74147).

Trip to the Alpe di Money (2,325 m/7,626 ft): departure point Valnontey; change in elevation 659 m (2,161 ft); time required 4 hours. A delight-

ful route with spectacular views of the circle of glaciers (Tribolazione, Gran Crou and Apostoli) and frequent encounters with herds of ibex and chamois.

Take the road at the bottom of the valley and then a wide bridle track on the right of the river. Passing the farmsteads at Valmiana, follow the path to the left which initially runs level along the hillside and then climbs towards the Alpe di Money. There is a longer but more beautiful return route. Instead of taking the same path back, continue in the opposite direction, past all the farmsteads, staying at the same height to encircle the head of the valley until you reach a bridge which crosses a stream flowing from the Gran Paradiso glacier.

Epinel – Alpe and Colle Trajo – Gran Nomenon chalets: departure point Epinel (hamlet in the Cogne valley, 1,452 m/4,762 ft); change in elevation 1,460 m (4,788 ft); time required 8 hours.

At Epinel descend towards the Gran Evvia river, cross it and begin climbing the opposite side by a steep path which winds through meadows and larches to the farmsteads of the Alpe Trajo (2,037 m/6,681 ft). Then comes another series of twists and turns among larches and rhododendrons to the Trajo hut (2,150 m/7,052 ft). Take the path along the ridge where the park kiosk stands, cross the Trajo river and follow the left bank to the valley which ends underneath the Colle del Trajo (2,877 m/9,436 ft). From here the path continues bending and spiralling upwards and eventually a flight of steps leads to the col, a strenuous climb rewarded by the view of the majestic and icy north face of the Grivola.

An easy but long, stony descent brings you, in an hour, to the Nomenon farmsteads (2,039 m/6,687 ft). You can return directly to the bottom of the valley, to the village of Vieyès (12 km/7½ miles from Cogne), or stay at altitude, taking a path constructed by the park authorities which links the Nomenon houses and the Trajo hut.

From the Barmasse refuge you descend to the Alpi Cortina di Sopra (rejoining path 13) and Cortina di Sotto (1,969 m/6,458 ft). Now begins the first climb of the day towards the Finestra d'Ersa (2,290 m/7,511 ft) which faces the Torgnon valley.

From the broad grassy ridge proceed north-west along the hillside and round the head of the valley, past the summer pastures of Vaéton, Zansuet and Drayère (up to here path 70, then path 71) until you come to the small Lake Tzan (2,482 m/8,141 ft; bivouac with 9 beds and cooking equipment). The name of the mountain which overlooks it to the south-west, Cima Bianca ("White Peak"), refers to the calcareous nature of the rock. This produces the karst phenomena of sinks, ravines and underground streams; in fact, about 20 minutes from the bivouac you can see where the Chavacour river vanishes under the surface.

If you do not need to stop, you can even bypass the bivouac and continue higher up on path 71; after about one hour's walk you reach Fenêtre de Tzan (2,734 m/8,967 ft; 4½ hours). You now enter the high valley of St Barthélemy, which you have to cross in order to get to the opposite side. From Fenêtre you take a zigzag path down to the Alpe Crottes (2,389 m/7,836 ft) and then continue down the valley alongside the stream to the Alpe Ollière valley. Here you leave the path which leads to Praz, cross the bridge over the stream and prepare for the longest and steepest climb of the stage: an uphill change in elevation of 650 m (2,132 ft). From La Serva alp (2,001 m/6,563 ft) you first go through the wood, then across meadows and rock ridges and finally up the west slope of the St Barthélemy valley to the top of the Freideront valley where, in a wild, rocky depression, the Santuario di Cuney (2,652 m/8,698 ft; 3½ hours) stands. You can stay the night in the refuge adjoining the sanctuary. Entrusted by the parish of St Barthélemy to the local section of the Italian Alpine Club (C.A.I.), it opens at weekends in July and August. (For information and confirmation of opening times tel. (0)165/767638; 12 beds.)

An alternative which cuts the long stage into two envisages an overnight stay at the Tzan mountain hut or at the next hut at Nebbia (2,590 m/8,495 ft), situated 100 m (100 yards) from Lake Luseney, at the head of the St Barthélemy valley (4 bunks). You reach this by walking for about half an hour up a

ALTA VIA NO. 2

On your arrival at Courmayeur after completing the Giants' Trail, you now have the possibility of returning by the delightful High-Level Walk No. 2 (*Alta Via No. 2*), known also as the Nature Trail because it includes several stages through the Gran Paradiso National Park. This itinerary is on the right side of the Val d'Aosta, starting at Val Veni and arriving at the Valle di Champocher, by way of the valleys of La Thuile, Grisenche, Rhêmes, Savaranche and Cogne. So it follows a broad loop which offers you glimpses of all the 4,000-m (13,120-ft) mountains of the Val d'Aosta, and can be broken down into fifteen stages. In addition to the eight of the Giants' Trail (*Alta Via N. 1*) there are another seven: Courmayeur – La Thuile (8½ hours); La Thuile – Val Grisenche (10 hours); Val Grisenche – Rhême Notre Dame (6 hours); Rhême Notre Dame – Eaux Rousses (6 hours); Eaux Rousses – Rifugio V. Sella (6 hours); Rifugio V. Sella – Cogne (3½ hours); and Cogne – Champocher (8 hours).

Opposite: many stretches of the Giants' Trail are totally wild and isolated.

Below: the ibex is always absolute master of the highest peaks.

steep path of the Alpe Crottes, an interesting diversion which is, in any event, a recommended variation of the standard route.

Santuario di Cuney to Dzovenno   E

5½ hours, change in elevation 550 m (1,804 ft) uphill, 1,650 m (5,412 ft) downhill

This stage leads to Valpelline through an area which for a long time was known only to the valley inhabitants and the odd walker or climber. The region constitutes a real outdoor museum, especially in the Lessona valley where you can come across eagles, chamois and a wealth of flowers. From Cuney you encircle the Becca di Fonteney, heading south as far as the ridge of the Col de Chaleby (2,683 m/8,800 ft; 2 hours); then you descend the grassy slopes to Val di

Breva, reach Pian Piscina sprinkled with countless small lakes, cross meadows towards the characteristic Dente Meridionale di Vessona and finally climb to the Colle di Vessona (2,789 m/9,148 ft; 2½ hours). At this point you are faced with the long and steep descent to the floor of the Valpelline, with its many points of natural interest. You walk along the Comba di Vessona, a narrow valley between the walls (subject to landslides) of the surrounding mountains, which in its lower section contracts into a spectacular gorge cut out by the Buthier river: the Betenda gorge (stone bridge dating from 1688).

The descent terminates at the bottom of the Valpelline, at Closé, one of the sixteen Oyace hamlets (1,457 m/4,779 ft; 2 hours). From here you must climb the road to Dzovenno (1.5 km/1 mile; 1,575 m/5,166 ft; food store; hotels Valentino,

The clouds that envelop the valley glisten in the light of dawn, a splendid sight that can only be enjoyed high up in the mountains.

THE GREAT ST BERNARD ROAD AND PASS

The story of mountain roads is closely associated with the geographical location and economy of the local populations. The Great St Bernard pass is an important example of this fact. Archaeological finds confirm that even before the time of the Salassi the pass was used by Neolithic people. Then the Salassi, a Celtic tribe which took over from the Liguri around 500 B.C., transformed the track into a road, building a refuge and erecting a statue to the god Pen. This later provided the name of the tract of the Alps from the Ferret pass to the Simplon (Pennine Alps).

The Romans subsequently paved the road, exchanged the statue of Pen for one of Jove and enlarged the refuge.

The pass was in fact known as Mont Joux or Monte Giove until the eleventh century when St Bernard of Menthon built his famous hospice there. This was destroyed by fire and rebuilt in the seventeenth century. The last time an army crossed the pass was in 1800 during Napoleon's second Italian campaign.

Part of the ancient track is still visible and an interesting day can be spent going over it and retracing the age-old route of the pilgrims, merchants and soldiers.

At the pass (2,473 m/8,111 ft) you can enjoy the hospitality of the four Augustinian monks who, assisted by other lay helpers, run a hotel which is even open in the winter when the snow prohibits road travel.

tel. (0)165/73901, and Meuble Dzovenno, tel. (0)165/73906).

Closé to Ollomont   H

7½ hours, change in elevation 1,035 m (3,375 ft) uphill, 1,380 m (4,526 ft) downhill

The valley of Valpelline, with the village of Valpelline (960 m/3,149 ft; 12 km/7½ miles from Aosta), divides into a Y shape; the main valley is to the right and continues as far as the artificial lake formed by the Place Mulin dam; the left branch leads to the Ollomont valley, once important for its copper mining.

The Valpelline is separated from the Ollomont valley by the long road that flanks Monte Morion. This sixth stage of the itinerary meets it at the Col de Breuson, thus linking Closé to Ollomont. The climb from Closé to the col is a very long one because the path makes a wide curve around the hill, past the alps of Eclève, Suchéaz and the Arp (2,195 m/7,193 ft) before reaching the slope leading up to the pass (2,492 m/8,173 ft). The descent is more direct, and Ollomont is reached after a diversion left to the Alpe del Berrio (1,923 m/6,307 ft). You can stay overnight in the only hotel in the village (1,356 m/4,447 ft; Mont Gelé, tel. (0)165/73220; 24 beds; food store).

Ollomont to Cuchepache   H

7¼ hours, change in elevation 1,450 m (4,756 ft) uphill, 1,100 m (3,608 ft) downhill

After Valpelline you come to the Great St Bernard valley, with its many villages and road leading to the Great St Bernard pass. This stage therefore takes you through country which is rather more heavily populated than the preceding ones and, in the final section, on roads.

Proceed from Ollomont on the road to the hamlet of Rey where a path forks off to the Alpe Champillon, crossed by the old "ru de By" irrigation canal. Over the canal continue right for the Tza Champillon pasture by way of the pass of that name which separates Monte Chenaille from the Crou de Blenche (2,708 m/8,882 ft; 3 hours).

Circling the south ridge of Monte Chenaille and passing the Alpe Pointier, you join the road which

climbs the Val de Menouvé, the left lateral branch of the Great St Bernard valley. At Bezet (1,630 m/5,346 ft; 2 hours) you leave the road and take the hill path above the valley, passing first the village of Eternod and then that of St Rhémy on the road leading to the pass (1,632 m/5,353 ft; 1¾ hours). From St Rhémy, finally, you cross the Artanavox river and continue on the level towards Laval and the road to Cuchepache (1,648 m/5,405 ft; ½ hour; Hôtel des Alpes; 24 beds; tel (0)165/78916).

Cuchepache to Courmayeur   H

8¾ hours, change in elevation 1,280 m (4,198 ft) uphill, 1,700 m (5,576 ft) downhill

This final stage is not too strenuous and provides many sweeping views over the Mont Blanc group

The warm colours of autumn in the Val d'Ayas announce the imminent arrival of winter and the mountain's long period of hibernation.

On pages 118 and 119: a typical alpine hut on a summer pasture high in the Val Ferret, near the end of the Giants' Trail.

from the Col Malatra, dominated by the peak itself, and along the Val Ferret.

From Cuchepache you proceed west, cross the road of the pass after Mottes, climb to Merdeux-Desot and enter the flat, green Comba di Merdeux, keeping to the left side. A last detrital slope leads up to the narrow opening of the Col Maratra (2,928 m/9,604 ft; 4 hours). The view from here is unique; ahead is the Grandes Jorasses group, to the left the massive dome of Mont Blanc, the jagged crest of Peuterey and the Aiguille Noire.

All that remains is the descent to Courmayeur. There are two possibilities. The first, which is more direct, is through the Val Ferret along the Malatra valley, joining the main road at Lavachey (1,642 m/5,385 ft). Walk along the edge of the road from Lavachey to Planpinieux and then take the track along the left side of the valley to Saxe, on the outskirts of Courmayeur (1,224 m/4,014 ft; stretch shared with the Tour du Mont Blanc; 4 hours; public bus service from Planpinieux to Courmayeur).

The second, longer but more satisfying, takes you higher above the Val Ferret by way of the terrace of the Mont de la Saxe. You get to this by leaving the main route above the Alpe di Malatra and crossing the Colle d'Entre Deux Sauts, the Col Sapin and the Testa Bernarda. You then come down directly to Courmayeur via the Rifugio Bertone (60 beds; tel. (0)165/89336) and the Val Sapin.

High-mountain detours. The route of the first three stages can be replaced by an alternative itinerary which is closer to the main Monte Rosa chain and goes via Breuil/Cervinia. Instead of crossing the Ayas and Valtournanche valleys with their respective villages, you traverse the heads of the valleys near to the glaciers. This is actually the initial section of the *Alta Via*, opened in 1977, but somewhat spoiled at the Col de Bettafuorca and the Colle delle Cime Bianche by pistes and the infrastructure of the Monterosa ski-carousel. Diff. H. **Alta Via no. 3:** This links the refuges of Monte Rosa, departure point for the ascent of the peaks on the Val d'Aosta side. It can constitute an alternative to the first three stages of the Giants' Trail, but because of the altitude and the icy surroundings it is reserved for expert trekkers (diff. EE). Route: Gressoney la Trinité – Rifugio Gnifetti (3,647 m/11,962 ft) – Rifugio Mezzalama (3,050 m/10,004 ft) – Breuil/Cervinia.

BERNINA TRAIL

In the central Alps, in the Engadine and the Valtellina

The Piz Bernina, the only 4,000-m (13,120-ft) peak in the Rhaetian Alps and the last of this altitude to the east, forms the apex of the Bernina chain which extends for 25 km (15½ miles) between Italy and Switzerland. On large-scale maps it is evident that the peaks of the Bernina group are surrounded by a series of deeply grooved valleys: the Valtellina to the south, the Val Poschiavo and Val Bernina to the east and the Upper Engadine to the north. To the west, beyond the Muretto Pass, the adjoining groups of the Monte Disgrazia and the Piz Badile are bounded by the valleys of the Mera (Val Bregaglia and Val Chiavenna).

The opposite sides of the Bernina group are structurally different. The southern section is characterized by a sequence of three shelves, across which are ranged successively Piz Tremoggia, the Piz Glüschaint group and the crowning ramparts of Piz Roseg (3,936 m/12,910 ft), Monte Scerscen (3,971 m/13,025 ft) and Piz Bernina (4,050 m/13,284 ft).

In contrast to the rocky spurs and buttresses of the southern side, the principal features of the northern sector are deep valleys, almost perpendicular to the watershed. Their basins are occupied by enormous glaciers with tongues that extend almost to the foot of the Upper Engadine, Bernina and Poschiavo valleys.

The scenery on the Swiss side, with the mountains and their glaciers which stretch down into the valleys, is quite spectacular. On the Italian side, the succession of jagged rock buttresses conceals until the last moment the sight of the higher mountains and

Useful addresses: Upper Engadine Tourist Office: Verkehrsverein Oberengadin, Pontresina, tel. 82.665.73 (Switzerland).
Maps: Carta Turistica Kompass, 1:50,000, no. 93 (Bernina-Sondrio); Landeskarte der Schweiz, 1:50,000, pp 268 (Julierpass), 269 (Berninapass), 279 (Brusio), 278 (M. Disgrazia).
Bibliography: G. Collomb, *Bernina Alps*, West Col Productions; K. Reynolds, *Walks in the Engadine*, Cumbria Press.

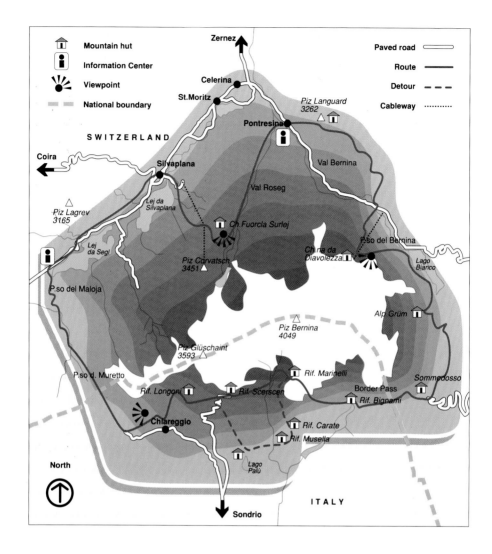

Distance: about 100 km (68 miles) divided into eight stages.
Departure and arrival points: Maloja Pass (1,815 m/5,953 ft) in the Grisons canton, Switzerland. The pass is linked to Milan by a motorway bus service (leaves from Piazza Castello; tel. (0)2/867631) and to St Moritz by the post services (from the railway station).
Where to stay: Maloja Pass (hotels and restaurants): Rifugio Surlej; Hotel Roseg; Pontresina (hotels and restaurants); Rifugio Languard; Rifugio Diavolezza;

Alp Grüm hotels; Rifugio Bignami; Rifugio Marinelli Bombardieri; Rifugio Longoni. All refuges are open from late June to early September.
Signposting: Direction signposts and red and white flags in Switzerland. Red/white/red flags and yellow triangles for the Alta Via della Val Malenco (stages 4, 5 and 6) in Italy.
Difficulty: Swiss side, R; Italian side H and E. In Switzerland you walk on well-marked paths and you can take cablecars every so often to reduce the distances and

get back down into the valleys. In Italy the route is through wilder surroundings and over rougher ground. On the traditional route, the easy crossing of the Caspoggio cirque glacier is included. The itinerary can be abandoned at the Campo Gera dam (stage 6; path to Campo Franscia and then the bus to Chiesa in Val Malenco) or at the Rifugio Longoni (road to San Giuseppe-Chiesa and path to Chiareggio).
When to go: July and August when all passes are free of snow.
Equipment: High altitude.

creates a landscape that is more segmented, wild and solitary. In Switzerland you can photograph Piz Bernina directly from the road along the valley floor or from any of the famous viewpoints that are reached by cable railway. In Italy, on the other hand, you have to walk considerable distances before coming to the Bocchette, where there is suddenly a splendid view of the line of high central peaks. Two contrasting faces, and two contrasting natural worlds which guarantee the walker making the Piz Bernina trek a succession of almost unrivalled scenic delights.

As regards the flora, the slopes of the Engadine are covered by conifer and mixed woods: larches on the left, birch and arolla pine on the right. But this woodland belt is restricted because above 2,000 m (6,500 ft) the landscape is of the alpine type, with grasslands and twisted, dwarf trees. This is typical of the upper Val Malenco where the vegetation includes many species gathered by the valley folk to make liqueurs and infusions: the alpine yarrow (*Achillea moscata*) and glacier wormwood (*Artemisia glacialis*). The scenic diversity of the Bernina group is completed by the innumerable lakes, large and small, which have been formed by the erosion of the surfaces by the great glaciers. Four huge lakes in the Upper Engadine are the sites of famous tourist resorts, and dozens of pools of varying dimensions are scattered about on the Italian side, at the edge of glaciers, in the heart of woods or among the rocks.

Summer pastures and mountain holidays

No less variegated than the geographical surroundings are the lives and activities of the people who live in the valleys at the foot of Piz Bernina.

The Upper Engadine, despite its altitude, ranging from some 1,800 m/5,900 ft on the Maloja Pass to about 1,700 m/5,575 ft on the Celerina, offers ideal surroundings for human settlement. Its particular south-west to north-east orientation, in fact, guarantees that both its slopes are warmed by the sun and encourage the establishment of villages. Moreover, the mountain chains which rise to 1,200–1,500 m (4,000–5,000 ft) above the valley floor protect it from the moist winds blowing both from the north and south, creating a climate which is unique in the Alps.

Add to all this a wealth of water, meadows and pastures, and it is easy to explain why many human

MAGGENGHI AND ALPEGGI

The traditional mountain way of life, in addition to agriculture and forestry, is reliant upon livestock rearing. This activity is conditioned by the lie of the land which has imposed a semi-nomadic life pattern taking people from the meadows around the villages to the mountain meadows and even higher to the *alpeggi*, the pastures accessible only in the summer.

The two traditional transhumance points in the Alps are the *maggengo*, between 1,300 and 1,500 m (c. 4,250–5,000 ft) and the *alpeggio*, between 1,500 and 2,200 m (c. 4,250–7,200 ft).

The *maggengo*, literally "May or first crop" – known in the Italian Alps also as *mayen*, *cassina*, *montagnette* and *stavoli*, in Switzerland as *Voralp* and in Austria as *Niederalp* – is the pasture midway up the mountain where the whole family spends the spring together with the livestock. In addition to a house built in wood or stone and made comfortable enough to live in, there is the cattle shed with an upper storey used as a hay loft to store the grass reaped from the fields which are also privately owned.

The high-mountain *alpeggio* – known also as *malga*, *alp*, *montagne*, *munt*, *tramal*, *tsa* and *casera* – is, by contrast, made up of a stretch of pasture and a few very simple and spartan dwellings. The hut (*balma* or *truna*) is often just a stone shelter designed to accommodate the men who bring up the animals in July and August. The alps may be privately or communally owned. In the former case the owner grazes his animals and those entrusted to him, in the latter the commune auctions the alps to the highest bidders or delegates the job to one individual who takes charge of the animals belonging to various owners. The Bernina itinerary passes a number of *alpeggi* that are organized in a variety of ways.

THE PARK OF THE POTHOLES

Before setting out on this walk, it is well worthwhile visiting the Nature Reserve of the Potholes, at the Maloja Pass. This is a wooded zone situated between the canton road and the ridge on which the nineteenth-century Belvedere Tower stands. There are some 30 potholes, known as Giants' Kettles, visible from a well-marked path and protected by fencing. The biggest of these (the largest being 11 m/36 ft deep and 16 m/52½ ft in circumference) are in the form of pools and bear the names of actual people who were associated with the pass at the end of the nineteenth century (e.g. the Waither pothole, named after the manager of the Hotel Kursaal, the Princess Maria Adelaide pothole, etc.).

Excavated in blocks of stratified gneiss with quartz veining, the potholes are a reminder of the presence of Quaternary glaciers which at one time covered the Engadine. They are in fact the result of erosion caused by the water of glacial rivers which poured into crevices, carrying pebbles that drilled away at the rocks on the bottom. Thus they gradually formed circular holes which, according to popular tradition, were artificial in origin: kettles dug out by giants for cooking.

The park covers 30 hectares (75 acres) and belongs to the Swiss League for the Protection of Nature.

settlements have sprung up around the basins formed by the streams in the lateral valleys: Isola, Silvaplana, Sils. St. Moritz and Pontresina are, on the other hand, typical terrace villages, the first on the slopes of Piz Nair, the second at the foot of Piz Muragl. From the architectural point of view, the most striking feature is the typical large house of plastered stone, its front decorated in sgraffito and embellished by bay windows. Its heart is the *stua*, a room entirely lined with wood and warmed by an enormous stove. Permanent homes have been built in the broad, luxuriant Val di Fex up to a height of 2,000 m (6,500 ft) linked by private roads to the valley, whereas usually at this altitude only summer pastures are to be found. It is to these pastures that the cooperatives bring the cattle to graze. All the operations associated with milk production are carried out here in the traditional long cattle sheds now equipped with modern machinery.

Farming and livestock rearing are still vital activities in the Engadine but they have necessarily taken second place to tourism which has developed apace since the nineteenth century.

Thanks to their favourable situation, villages have been able to expand with the building of hotels and villas, while funiculars, rack and pinion railways and chairlifts have been constructed everywhere to carry winter sports enthusiasts up and down the slopes with the maximum efficiency and convenience. Walking in the Upper Engadine and its lateral Bernina valley therefore takes you through a region that has been heavily developed to cater for the influx of tourism on an international scale, but by and large the trail will show how the resorts do not disturb the natural features. Things are very different, however, on the southern side of the Bernina chain where our itinerary goes through the upper Val Malenco.

No more tourist centers, roads, cablecars – just the silence of the mountain broken only by the wind and the tinkling bells of grazing cattle. During the three-day trek you pass only three alpine refuges, departure points for the ascent of the particular mountains, and a series of summer pastures starting from a height of 2,000 m (6,500 ft): Gembrè, Fellaria, Fora, dell'Oro. These are actually temporary summer villages consisting of buildings for various purposes. The large number of *baite*, huts faced with stone and a roof of slate tiles, testify to the fact that the pasture

was exploited individually and each family who brought up the animals, had their own, albeit primitive, house.

Although there are signs everywhere that these mountain activities, which involve a good deal of hardship, are being abandoned, you can still see the various stages of milk production with the use of traditional instruments such as water and hand churns, cheese presses, etc.

The itinerary

The Bernina Trail makes a complete circuit of the Bernina group of the Central Alps, departing and arriving in Switzerland at the Maloja Pass (in the Grisons canton). The first part of the route is along the north side of the chain in the Upper Engadine and in the Bernina and Poschiavo valleys; the second part is in Italy, in the upper Val Malenco (Valtellina).

Above: the lower Scerscen glacier with the slopes of the Glüschaint and Sella peaks in the background.

On pages 124 and 125: the southern side of the Bernina group with the Forbici lake in the foreground.

THE WORLD OF THE LADINS

The Val Poschiavo and the Engadine belong to the canton of Grisons (Graubünden). Whereas the first is Italian-speaking and follows Italian traditions, the second has a population of Ladin traditions. The bilingual road signs (in Ladin and German) are a reminder that this is another world, to which the Romans brought their civilization through the unifying force of Latin but which, at a later time, came under German influence.

The latter achieved predominance in the past couple of centuries as a result of economic development (roads, railways, tourism), transforming even the names: thus the Ladin San Murezzan was replaced by that of St. Moritz, and the Italian Passo del Maloggia (the ancient spring pasture of the Val Bregaglia) became the Maloja Pass.

In the Bernina area Swiss maps therefore give the Ladin place names and it is useful to be familiar with the main terms in order to interpret the maps:

Acla	Small group
Isla	Island
Fuorcla	Fork
Chamanna	Hut
Chesa	House
Corn	Horn, peak
Crasta	Crest
Funtauna	Spring
God	Wood
Lej	Lake
Margun	Dairy
Uva	River
Pas-chura	Pasture
Plan	Plain
Punt	Bridge
Senda	Path
Stradella	Path
Tegia	Alpine hut

The term *vadret*, derived from the Latin *nix veterata* (old snow), means glacier (Vadret da Tschierva, etc.). Translated into Italian, the term *vedretta* is also applied to glaciers on the southern slopes.

The first section is easier because there are skilifts and cablecars and villages near the trail in the valley. The second is more strenuous as it crosses more isolated and wilder mountain terrain.

The total distance is about 110 km (68 miles), divided into eight stages. The overall gain in height is about 4,000 m (13,120 ft).

Maloja to Fuorcla Surlej R

4¼ hours, change in elevation 1,150 m (3,772 ft) uphill, 200 m (655 ft) downhill

The Engadine Way is a long path which links the Maloja Pass to St. Moritz; it runs through larch woods and meadows on the left side of the valley, with good views everywhere of the lakes below.

We follow the first part from the Maloja Pass (directional signpost outside the village) to the fork after the Grupin where the path bears right in its descent to Silvaplana (3 hours). One of the interest-

ing features along this section is the *maggesi*, the spring pastures, of Blaunca and Grevasalvas.

At Silvaplana you cross the valley and climb the opposite side to the Corvatch cableway station. The cablecar takes you up to the intermediate station of Murtel (2,699 m/8,852 ft) where you resume the journey on foot. You come down gradually, heading westward, and then continue along the hillside across the head of the valley where the lake, Lej da Fuorcla, is situated. Passing the lateral moraines and stream of the Vadrec da Corvatsch, you then take the path coming up from the valley and climb the slope which leads to the pass (½ hour).

If you do not wish to take the cablecar, there is a farm road to the right of the station which winds its way up to the alp and to the Margun Surlej (2,272 m/7,452 ft). From here you take a marked path around the spur of Piz Murtel and rejoin the itinerary just below the Fuorcla Surlej, after reclimbing the Lej da Fuorcla valley (3 hours). The Fuorcla Surlej

Below: the village of Silvaplana, situated on a cone which encloses the Lej da Silvaplana.

THE HIGHEST RAILWAY IN EUROPE

"The transalpine Grisons route from Tirano in Valtellina to St. Moritz in the Engadine: an unforgettable journey from south to north across time and space." This is how a Swiss publicity leaflet describes the Bernina Railway (photograph below) which, without a cogwheel, negotiates slopes with a 70 per cent gradient, travelling across the Bernina Pass at a height of 2,253 m (7,390 ft). One of the most extraordinary stretches is the spiral ramp of Brusio, but the entire journey provides a succession of wonderful sights due above all to the contrast of the dark greenery of the woods against the dazzling whiteness of the glaciers. To enjoy the mountain scenery for a longer period, you can alight at one of the intermediate stations and tackle a section of the trip on foot or climb up to a viewpoint.

From the Bernina–Lagalp and Bernina–Diavolezza stations two trains run to the summit of Piz Lagalp and to Rifugio Diavolezza respectively. The view is dominated by the elegant north wall of Piz Palü, notable for its three challenging

crests of rock and ice. The funicular for Muotta Muragl leaves from the Punt Muragl station, while Piz Nair can be reached from St. Moritz by funicular and cablecar. Both offer magnificent views over the entire Upper Engadine from St. Moritz to the Maloja, while the Languard zone provides the most spectacular sights of the central Bernina group with Piz Bernina, Monte Scerscen and Piz Roseg.

Itineraries that link one station to another include the following paths: Pontresina–St. Moritz (1 hour), Ospizio Bernina–Alp Grüm (1 hour) and Alp Grüm–Cavaglia (¾ hour).

In winter the train serves cross-country skiers who use the pistes traced alongside the railway, while tourists have at their disposal a horse-drawn sledge service from Pontresina up the Val Roseg to the hotel of that name which skirts the cross-country pistes.

There is a daily service to Tirano where connections leave for Milan and St. Moritz (the Bernina Express).

(2,755 m/9,036 ft) is a broad saddle between Piz Murtel and Monte d'Arlas, which derives its name from the village of Surlej beneath (sur Lej from the Latin *super lacum*, "above the lake of Silvaplana"). It provides the most convenient passage from the Upper Engadine to the Val Roseg, an offshoot of the Val Bernina, and is an excellent viewpoint over the cirque glaciers of Roseg and Tschierva, the former in the Sella–Glüschaint range, the latter in the Piz Bernina–Monte Scerscen–Piz Roseg triad, mirrored in the tiny lake on the western side. Here there is a hotel, (60 beds; tel. 82.663.03 [Switzerland]).

Fuorcla Surlej to Rifugio Languard R

5 hours, change in elevation 980 m (3,214 ft) uphill, 1,200 m (3,936 ft) downhill

From Fuorcla Surlej you lose height rapidly and eventually reach a junction on the side of the Val Roseg. On the right you go up the valley hillside to the mountain hut, Rifugio Coaz, departure point for the ascents of the Sella–Glüschaint group. Continue by descending to the left to the Hotel Roseg (1,999 m/6,556 ft), linked to Pontresina by a road closed to traffic and used in summer only by horse-drawn carriages. Descend the valley again, first walking on the road and then on the path on its right side which ends at the railway station (1,774 m/5,818 ft; 2 hours). You have now arrived at the large tourist resort of Pontresina, the only village in the Bernina valley. The valley branches off in a south-easterly direction from the principal valley of the Enn between Celerina and Samaden to the Bernina pass.

From Pontresina use the chairlift which takes you in a quarter of an hour to the Alp Languard (2,201 m/7,219 ft). From here the path climbs to the old horse station (Rosstation) and continues for long stretches along the hillside, with some steep bends on the right side of the Languard valley and leading to the base of the rocky crag of Piz Languard. When you come to the junction ignore the path on the right and take the zigzag trail upward to the Georgy Hütte (3,200 m/10,496 ft; 2½ hours) just below the summit of Piz Languard. The hut is open from the end of June to early October, with 20 beds in a dormitory. After a well-earned rest you will be ready for the short climb (15 minutes) to the top, an incomparable spot for views of the rising or setting sun.

ENGADINE MUSEUMS

Even the most hurried visit to the Upper Engadine must allow time for a look at the two museums in St. Moritz. The first is dedicated to Giovanni Segantini, the Italian painter who from 1894 to 1899 lived on the Maloja Pass and is buried in the cemetery there.

His works, and in particular the oil triptych *La Vita, La Natura e La Morte*, reproduce, with unequalled insight and imagination, the peculiar light and atmosphere of the mountains he loved. He met his death, cut off by a snowstorm, in his solitary Schanferg hut, 3,000 m (9,840 ft) up on the slopes of Piz Muragl, where he had chosen to retreat in order to complete his last masterpiece. The museum is situated on the Champfer road in a domed building of 1909 (entry fee; closed on Mondays, in May and in November).

The second, Engadiner Museum/ Museum Engiadinais, is in a 1906 building in the style of an Engadine house and contains a large historical and ethnographic collection. The exhibits include prehistoric finds, objects associated with the ancient iron mines and a series of traditional costumes. The most interesting part of the museum, however, consists of faithful reproductions of the interiors of farm houses and buildings (entrance fee; closed in May and November).

On the way from Pontresina in the course of stage 2 of the itinerary, it is worth visiting the recent Alpine Museum, set up in an old building which has retained much of its original furniture. There are sections devoted to birds and glaciology. The interior of an Alpine Club refuge has also been reconstructed.

Piz Languard to Rifugio Diavolezza   **R**

5 hours (3 hours with cablecar), change in elevation 1,100 m (3,508 ft) uphill, 880 m (2,886 ft) downhill

From the hut descend to the junction below where a diversion to the left takes you on a lengthy trek along the hillside under the Languard ridge and then heads south-east towards the Fuorcla Pischa (2,874 m/9,426 ft; 1 hour). You are now in the heart of the reserve for the protection of alpine flowers, a wild botanical garden covering the slopes of the Piz Languard and the Val da Fain. At Fourcla Pischa (with a fine view of the small Pischa lakes below), you leave the direct path to the Fuorcla Pruna to your left and take the one on the right which, still heading south-east across stony terrain, leads to the Fuorcla S (2,970 m/9,741 ft; ½ hour). This is a stretch which may pose orienta-

Marmots, those attractive and playful rodents, are often to be seen out in the open, along both the Swiss and Italian stretches of path.

Left: the Blanca and Grevasalvas magesi (spring pastures) overlook Lake Sils.

tion difficulties when visibility is poor. The path winds sharply down to the grasslands on the western side of the valley, a zone densely populated by marmots, on the right of the Ova Pischa which flows from the lake above, and joins up with the cart track of the Val da Fain. Continuing down the first part of this track by way of the Alp Bernina (2,117 m/6,943 ft), you reach the Bernina road between the Bernina Suot railway station (below) and the station (above) from which the cablecars climb to the Diavolezza, reached in a few minutes on foot by bearing left along the road or by a longer route on the path which winds through the meadows (1 km; 1½–3 hours).

The next port of call is Rifugio Diavolezza – which is reached either by walking up the path beside the cableway (2 hours) or by taking the cablecar itself. The refuge has 186 beds (tel. 82.662.05

Signpost in the Engadine.

The Alpe Fora falls near Rifugio Longoni (Alta Val Malenco).

[Switzerland]) and is the departure point for the ascent of Piz Palü which, with its three characteristic crests, is one of the most spectacular and challenging rock walls in the Alps. The most rewarding viewpoint is Munt Pers (3,207 m/10,518 ft) which may be climbed easily from the refuge, making for the large south-eastern ridge (1 hour).

Rifugio Diavolezza to Alp Grüm   R

3½ hours, change in elevation 880 m (2,886 ft) downhill only

From Rifugio Diavolezza you descend the path again, but below the Diavolezza lake, instead of making for the cablecar departure station, you bear right along the side of the Arlas valley, passing the tiny Lej d'Arlas, eventually rejoining the railway and road at Lej Pitchen (2,221 m/7,285 ft; 1½ hours). At the junction turn right along the south-west shore of Lej Nair and Lago Bianco, at the foot of Piz Cambrena and Piz d'Arlas. The railway line runs along the opposite shore. A little higher up is the Bernina Pass hostel (2,307 m/7,567 ft; 30 beds; tel.

82.503.03 [Switzerland]). This is an area of great natural interest on the watershed between the basins of the Mediterranean and the Black Sea.

The narrow strip of land which separates Lago Bianco and Lej Nair causes the water flowing from the northern face of Piz Cambrena to empty partly into the former lake and partly into the latter. Lago Bianco has its outlet in Val di Pila (Acqua di Pila) and in the Cavagliasco river which is a tributary of the Poschiavino. Its waters therefore form part of the Po and Mediterranean basins.

Lej Nair, however, has its outlet in the Ova da Bernina, an affluent of the Enn and thus a tributary of the Danube and the Black Sea.

As may be gleaned from the place names, the Bernina pass marks the dividing line between two different languages: Ladin to the north, in the Engadine, and Italian to the south, in Val Poschiavo. And you now come down into Val Poschiavo itself, immediately after the end of Lago Bianco, following the old trade route of the Bernina pass. Turn right at the first junction, on the east side of the Sassal Mason, climbing gently to the top where, from the restaurant (2,355 m/7,724 ft), there is an incomparable view of the Palü cirque glacier. Further on you make a number of downward turns, heading back east to the railway and following its track as far as the Alp Grüm (2,091 m/6,858 ft; 2 hours; three hotels).

Near the station it is worth visiting the small botanical garden with some 3,000 varieties of alpine flora.

Alp Grüm to Rifugio Bignami   H

5½ hours, change in elevation 1,150 m (3,772 ft) uphill, 800 m (2,624 ft) downhill

This is a frontier crossing stage. From the Alp Grüm you come down across the railway tracks to the broad plain of the Alpe Cavaglia (1,963 m/6,438 ft). Head right towards Cavagliola and then proceed through the Ghiblung wood on the right slope of Piz Varuna. You reach the Stabil di Varuna beyond which you cross the Varuna valley (bridge over the rapid), past the Bosch da Braita and eventually meet the road from Poschiavo. Continue up this for a while to Somdoss (2,160 m/7,085 ft). Now begins the most strenuous part of the stage – the climb up the Val Ursè, at first on the left side, followed by a long walk along the hillside among rocks and detritus to the

---

CROSS-COUNTRY SKIING

Because of the flat lie of the land, the Engadine is an ideal place for practising cross-country skiing. Every village has its own well-maintained cross-country tracks and a cross-country ski center where you can prepare your skis and stop for a hot drink and a break. The most famous sporting fixture is the Engadina Ski Marathon which is held annually in March over a course of 42 km (26 miles), from the Maloja Pass to Zuoz, in which more than 10,000 skiers take part. However, if you prefer to enjoy the scenery at leisure, there is an exceptional piste, interlinking all the training tracks, which extends for about 100 km (62 miles) from the Maloja Pass to the border between Austria and Switzerland at Martina. It can be broken down into three convenient stages: Stage 1: Maloja Pass–St. Moritz along the icy surface of the lakes; St. Moritz–Pontresina over the rise of the Lej da Staz; Pontresina–Samaden–Zuoz on the level valley floor (42 km/26 miles; Ski Marathon course).

Stage 2: Zuoz–Zernez–Giarsun (33 km/20 miles; Loipa Engiadina). This is a narrow stretch through the valley from the Upper to Lower Engadine and the piste has more ups and downs, some of them fairly steep. From Giarsun to Scuol the Ardez gorges block the way and there is a short transfer by train.

Stage 3: Scuol–Martina (22 km/13½ miles). The track is slightly downhill, along the banks of the Inn and through the splendid woods, first of conifers, then of broadleaved trees, until you reach Martina, the frontier with Austria (900 m/2,952 ft) (course of the Passlung race). Post buses and trains link all the departure and arrival points of the three stages.

THE ENGADINE NATIONAL PARK

This is the oldest national park in Europe, having been opened in 1914 to provide students with a vast area of scientific research. It covers an enormous area of 169 km² (65 sq. miles) across the Fuorn Pass (Ofenpass) which links the Upper Engadine with the Val Monastero. It contains several dolomitic mountains of more than 3,000 m (9,850 ft) with a series of deep, narrow valleys branching off from their foothills.

The park may be divided into three zones of differing geographical character: in the north the Val Scharl sector centers upon Scuol; the central Fuorn–Val Mustair sector has a common boundary with the Stelvio National Park (Livigno and Cancano lakes); to the west is the Val Cluozza sector.

The tree vegetation (photograph below) consists mainly of Norway spruce (*Picea excelsa*), which is replaced above 2,000 m (6,500 ft) by arolla pine (*Pinus cembra*) and European larch (*Larix decidua*). Higher still is the mountain pine (*Pinus mugo*), covering an area of some 25 km² (9 ½ sq. miles). Among the many animals are chamois, ibex, red deer and roe deer.

Access and Information Centers: National Park House, Zernez (35 km/22 miles from St. Moritz; tel. 82.813.78 [Switzerland]) open 2 June to 25 October. Information, exhibitions, slide projections and films.

Itineraries: As the park serves as an actual laboratory, much of the park is out of bounds to visitors. But there are paths for tourists to follow with information and facilities. It is forbidden to stray from these. Two itineraries leave from Il Fuorn hotel (1,794 m/5,884 ft, tel. 82.812.26 [Switzerland]), the only tourist facility inside the park, on the Zernez–Ofenpass motor road (post bus stop). They are marked by signposts and red

and white flags. It is advisable to carry binoculars. Best period: mid-May to mid-October.

Fuorn–Munt la Schera–Buffalora–Fuorn

4½ hours, change in elevation 792 m (2,597 ft) uphill.

This is one of the most beautiful, varied and rewarding routes in the park, departing from carpark no. 5 just below the hotel.

It may be broken down into three stages. The first comprises a climb up the hill to the Alp la Schera (2,091 m/6,858 ft; park ranger observation post), beyond which you leave the path for Buffalora and take the left turn to climb up to the summit of Munt la Schera (2,586 m/8,482 ft; exceptional viewpoint over the park and the Italian Livigno and Gallo valleys). The second stage involves a long walk over the hillside through meadows to the dome of Munt Buffalora (1,630 m/5,346 ft) and then a descent to the bottom of the valley at the Buffalora restaurant. The third stage takes you back to the Fuorn along an easy path which runs beside the Ova da Fuorn road.

Fuorn–Val da Stabelchod–Margunet–Val da Botsch–Fuorn

3 hours, change in elevation 540 m (1,771 ft) uphill.

A shorter walk than the previous one but steeper and more strenuous, through a wild, rocky landscape. From the hotel you climb the valley path to carpark no. 9. Here you leave the path for Buffalora, bear left, go past the Stabelchod park refuge and climb the enclosed valley (a stretch of the path is artificial and protected by chains) up to the Margunet plain (2,328 m/7,635 ft, observation of deer herds). This is the watershed between the Val da Stabelchod and the Val da Botsch, and you now head down towards the valley path and from there to the hotel.

pass which marks the border between Switzerland and Italy (2,628 m/8,620 ft; 4 hours).

From the pass you come down through meadows to the Alpe Gembrè below, now largely abandoned; continue right by the path encircling the huge artificial basin of the Campo Gera dam, cross the rivers flowing in a cascade from the tongues of the eastern and western Fellaria cirque glaciers above, and climb the zigzag path to the terrace of the Bignami hut (2,401 m/7,875 ft; 1½–5½ hours). This refuge, owned by the Milan section of the Alpine Club, has 60 beds (tel. (0)342/451178 [Italy]).

Capanna Bignami to Rifugio Marinelli Bombardieri   E

3 hours, change in elevation 700 m (2,296 ft) uphill, 300 m (984 ft) downhill

This is the shortest stage of the Bernina Trail but it takes you into the midst of the southern-face glaciers of the group. The most direct route thus entails descending the Caspoggio cirque glacier which, apart from the climb up the final crevasse, presents no difficulties. From the hut you make for the nearby Alpe di Fellaria, cross a river and once more climb the valley, the last cirque of which, as it nears the Bocchetta di Caspoggio, is occupied by a glacier. From the Bocchetta (2,983 m/9,784 ft), which opens out between the Cima di Fellaria and the Cima di Caspoggio, you make an easy descent to the right across the cirque glacier to its lateral moraines. Here you take the path leading from the Rifugio Carate and make a long, winding climb to the panoramic terrace with the Rifugio Marinelli Bombardieri (2,813 m/9,226 ft; 3 hours; 200 beds; tel. (0)342/451454 [Italy]).

Rifugio Marinelli Bombardieri to Rifugio Longoni   E

5 hours, change in elevation 600 m (1,968 ft) uphill, 550 m (1,804 ft) downhill

This is the wildest and most solitary part of the itinerary, not too arduous as regards changes of level but nevertheless a long route which entails crossing moraines and valleys along none too well-marked tracks. Good visibility is therefore essential. Before leaving, find out from the management of the refuge

what the condition of the bridges across the rivers is, and whether the route should be varied.

From the Rifugio Marinelli descend the path off the Belvedere terrace to the left moraine of the upper Scerscen glacier with its towering serac. Cross the bridges over two raging torrents and then, following the line of the central moraine, descend into the valley, once occupied by the upper and lower Scerscen glaciers which are now situated higher up.

Cross another river by its bridge and climb the facing valley leading to the Forcella d'Entova (2,381 m/7,810 ft). Descend the opposite side to a small lake covered permanently with ice and a terrace which is the terminating point of a paved road from San Giuseppe (Chiesa in Val Malenco). Follow it for a few kilometers to a hairpin bend (signposted) and take the path on the right up to the Rifugio Longoni (2,450 m/8,036 ft; Seregno Alpine Club; 30 beds: tel. (0)342/451120 [Italy]).

Above: making butter with a traditional churn on the Alpe Poschiavina.

Rifugio Longoni to Passo del Maloja

5½ hours, change in elevation 600 m (1,968 ft) uphill, 1,200 m (3,936 ft) downhill

On pages 138 and 139: the northern side of the Bernina group; from the left, three spectacular peaks, Piz Bernina, Monte Scerscen and Piz Roseg with the Vadret da Schierva.

Go down from the refuge to the Alpe Fora and follow the hillside path that goes round the southern slopes of Piz Fora. Instead of taking the path down to the village of Chiareggio (signposted junction), keep high above the valley as far as the edge of the wood, reaching the Alpe dell'Oro (2,010 m/6,593 ft; 2 hours). The scenery along the way is dominated by the great chain of Monte Disgrazia, with marvellous views of its grandiose, icy north wall. At the alp there is a military road from Chiareggio, constructed during the First World War; this soon becomes a path which leads through the narrow valley up to the Muretto Pass situated between Monte del Forno and Monte Muretto (2,582 m/8,469 ft; 1½ hours). You are now on one of the principal trade routes of former days, the quickest means of communication between the Valtellina and the Upper Engadine, used by mules laden with casks of wine and *piode* – smooth slabs of rock utilized as roofing tiles. From the pass you come down a path in Swiss Val Muretto to the alp and beautiful lake of Cavloc (on the left is a path which leads to the Forno glacier). Follow the road from here to the Maloja Pass (1,815 m/5,953 ft; 2 hours).

Opposite: a winter view of the River Sela with the little church of Segl Baselgia in the Upper Engadine.

Below: a typical grotto of the Val Poschiavina, used by the shepherds to keep the products of the summer pastures cool.

DOLOMITES HIGH-LEVEL WALK NO. 1

Alta Via N. 1

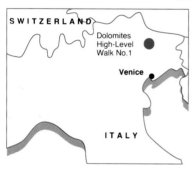

The Dolomites, a range of mountains lying in the Trentino-Alto Adige and Veneto regions of Northern Italy, were once known as the "pale mountains" because of the particular coloration they take on at the magic hour of sunset. They cover a vast area, divided geographically into two sectors, the western and eastern Dolomites, separated by the Val Cordevole and the Val Badia. The former includes, among others, the mountains of the Sella group, the Pale di San Martino and Marmolada, which at 3,343 m (10,965 ft) is the highest in the Dolomites. The latter includes the groups of Marmole, Tre Cime di Laveredo (Drei Zinnen), Antelao, Tofane, Civetta and Schiara, all mountains famous for their rugged beauty and allure to mountain climbers and trekkers the world over. The itinerary described here was the first to be laid out in the region. It takes you through the eastern Dolomites, running from north to south, and enables you to see much of the area's most characteristic scenery, including the Tofane, Civetta and Schiara ranges. You walk through dense forests of larch and fir at heights of up to 2,000 m (6,500 ft); and higher still through luxuriant pastures and thickets of mugo pine which grow on the heaps of rubble along the typical scree slips. With the vertical rock walls looming above, this dramatic scenery has been the inspiration for many local legends.

Useful addresses: Ente Provinciale per il Turismo, Belluno, Via R. Pesaro, 21, tel. (0)437/940083; Club Alpino Italiano, Belluno section, Via Ricci, 1, Belluno. Azienda di Soggiorno e di Turismo, Dobbiaco BZ, tel. (0)474/72132.
Maps: Carta Turistica Kompass, 1:50,000, pp 55, 67, 77; Carta dei rifugi e dei sentieri delle Dolomiti Tabacco (refuges and paths in Dolomites); pp 1 and 4; Carte Edizioni Geografica di Primiero, scale 1:25,000, p. 010; scale 1:50,000, p. 1.
Bibliography: M. Collins, *Alta Via – High-Level Walks in the Dolomites*, Cicerone Press; *Alta Via no. 1*, Ente Provinciale del Turismo di Belluno, four-language edition.

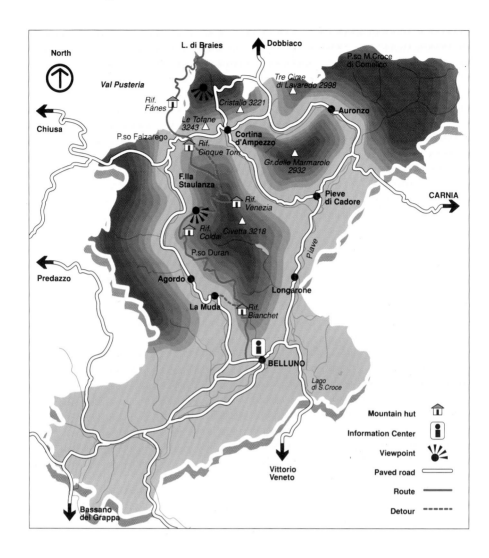

Distance: 130 km (80 miles), divided into ten stages.

Departure point: Lago di Braies (Val Pusteria [Pustertal], province of Bolzano in the Trentino-Alto Adige); bus service from Villabassa or Monguelfo (both stations on the Fortezza–Brunico – S. Candido railway line). Fortezza on main north-south railway line and autostrada.

Arrival point: Belluno (Veneto). If you want to leave your car at the departure point, you can return from Belluno to Braies by bus from the bus station.

Where to stay: There are many refuges, both privately owned and belonging to sections of the Italian Alpine Club (CAI), along the first part of the route. During the crowded summer months advance booking is essential, particularly for large groups. You also cross main roads that in case of emergency will take you down to the villages in the valley (Cortina d'Ampezzo, Zoldo Alto, Agordo). The final Schiara section, however, is more secluded and refuges are farther apart (e.g. Carestiato, Pramperet,

Bianchet). The majority of *rifugi* are open from June to September.

Signposting: The official sign of the *Alta Via N. 1* is a blue triangle with the number 1 in it; Italian Alpine Club (CAI) signs are red/white/red and blue/red flags with path numbers.

When to go: End June, July, August and first half September.

Difficulty: For the basic itinerary described, H. This is by way of paths, tracks and dirt roads, and only occasionally using fitted safety devices.

Equipment: High altitude.

Local languages and traditions

The Dolomites represent a meeting point of three different civilizations whose worlds are linked by the stages of this trail. The journey starts in the province of Bolzano, where a typically Austrian atmosphere prevails and the people speak German and a dialect of South Tyrol. It then touches the valleys populated by Ladins, notably around the Sella group and adjacent zones, and finally reaches the Belluno province where Italian and a Veneto dialect is spoken. And the surroundings of the *Alta Via*, not surprisingly, reflect these changes as it winds its way through the different areas.

In the northern and central sectors, tourism has made its indelible mark, with main roads and a vast network of minor roads leading to the lateral valleys. Hikers can easily find accommodation in the many hotels and *rifugi* or *Hütten*; the mountain huts are often also accessible with a four-wheel drive vehicle. In the Tofane and Nuvolau areas cablecars and chairlifts will carry tourists conveniently up to the mountain viewpoints to avoid unnecessary fatigue. Not far away, furthermore, are the major tourist resorts of the Val Pusteria, Val d'Ampezzo (Cortina) and Val Cordevole (Alleghe). South of the Civetta group, on the other hand, you find a much more sparsely populated and less frequented part of the Dolomites, the Schiara region.

The itinerary

High-Level Walk no. 1, the first of its kind to be planned and opened in the Dolomites, links Braies (in Alto Adige) to Belluno (in Veneto). The basic route avoids crossing Schiara at the end because this would present difficulties to inexperienced climbers. It is about 130 km (80 miles) long, divided into ten stages, and can be tackled by virtually any hiker with a minimal experience of mountain environments. The paths are clearly visible and signposted. There are numerous places for resting so that you can measure out and plan the route according to your abilities and requirements. Including inevitable stops, the itinerary takes about 15 days. The basic route, however, can be lengthened as you wish to take in various detours. The total change in elevation, up and down, is about 5,850 m (19,190 ft).

THE ALPINE FLORA

At the end of the last Ice Age, about 25,000 years ago, the progressive retreat of the glaciers and the improvement in climatic conditions permitted vegetation to colonize the highest mountain regions. The variety of the plant species is determined by many factors but primarily it depends on altitude. The following represents the distribution of altimetric zones in the Alps:

A Sub-montane zone
1. Mediterranean zone
   0–100 m (0–330 ft)
2. Sub-Mediterranean zone
   100–400 m (330–1,310 ft)
3. Sub-montane zone
   400–800 m (1,310–2,625 ft)
B Montane zone
4. Lower montane zone
   800–1,400 m (2,625–4,600 ft)
5. Upper montane zone
   1,400–2,000 m (4,600–6,560 ft)
C High alpine zone
6. Sub-alpine zone
   2,000–2,400 m (6,560–7,875 ft)
7. Alpine zone
   2,400–2,700 m (7,875–8,855 ft)
Snow line
8. High alpine zone
   2,700–3,000 m (8,855–9,850 ft)
9. Snow zone   peaks

In each zone the various species are ecologically balanced with their surroundings. At each level, nevertheless, there are variations according to temperature, rainfall, sunlight, snowfall and nature of the soil. Typical of soils rich in calcium, i.e. deriving from predominantly calcareous rocks as are to be found in the Eastern Alps, is the mugo pine (*Pinus mugo mugo*), while on the same biotic level, on siliceous soils originating from crystalline rocks typical of the Western Alps, one finds the mountain pine (*Pinus montana*) with clumps of myrtle (*Vaccinium myrtillus*) and rhododendron (*Rhododendron*).

CASTELLETTO AND THE UNDERGROUND TUNNEL

During the First World War the Dolomites were the scene of bitter engagements between the opposing armies. Fighting took place in alpine surroundings which were only usually braved by climbers. Many mountains were thus transformed into real natural fortresses: shelters were constructed on narrow rock ledges and artillery emplacements on peaks (a cannon was hoisted by the Italians to the top of Monte Popera), and tunnels excavated through rock with a view to surprising and blowing up enemy fortifications. Those troops not killed in the fighting succumbed during the long, freezing winter months to exposure and avalanches. There are many memorials all along the *Alta Via* to the "white war" of 1915–18.

One of the most daring exploits was the excavation of an underground tunnel at Castelletto (Schreckenstein or Sasso del Terrore, "the tragic rock"), the south-western spur of the Tofana di Rozes from which the Austrians bombarded the Italian lines of the Val Costeana. After vain attempts at assailing this prized observation point, the Italians dug a tunnel and on 11 July 1916 used 35 tonnes of gelignite to blow up the center of the Austrian defenses and capture the position.

The tunnel, today rebuilt and restored, can be visited as a variant of stage 3. From the Forcella di Bos you leave the main itinerary and follow the path which runs beneath the south wall of the Tofana di Rozes and leads to the base of the tunnel. The entrance is high up and you have to climb a low wall with ropes and metal ladders. The tunnel is 500 m (1,640 ft) long and zigzags up into the heart of the mountain (wooden steps and rails) gaining 100 m (100 yards) in height. It emerges immediately after the crater made by the explosion in 1916. You return to the Forcella di Bos along another path fitted with climbing aids. A torch and climbing experience are essential: difficulty EE.

Lago di Braies to Rifugio Biella   H

6 km (3¾ miles), 3½ hours, change in elevation 695 m (2,280 ft) uphill, 60 m (197 ft) downhill

A short transfer stage which leads from the broad, lush Val Pusteria to the true world of the Dolomites. The walk begins in the Val di Braies which opens southward between Monguelfo and Villabassa. The actual point of departure is the hotel on the Lago di Braies (Hotel Pragser Wildsee; 1,494 m/4,900 ft; 220 beds; tel. (0)474/78602) which can be reached by car or the public bus service.

From the hotel you walk around the west side of the lake, past the start of the Val Foresta. At the southern end you climb a valley dominated by Croda del Becco as far as the final cirque (Gorn/Ofenkar) where the path sharply winds up the last slope leading to Porta Sora 'i Forn (small chapel, 2,388 m/7,832 ft).

The strenuous part of this section is now over. So there is time to admire the wonderful view before coming down to Rifugio Biella situated just underneath the pass in Veneto territory (province of Belluno).

Rifugio Biella (Seekofelhütte; 2,327 m/7,632 ft; tel. (0)436/866991) has 35 bunk beds and is linked to Sennes by a track.

Rifugio Biella to Rifugio Fanes   R

15.5 km (9½ miles), 4½ hours, change in elevation 510 m (1,673 ft) uphill, 786 m (2,578 ft) downhill

An easy transfer stage, for the most part on unpaved tracks, also suitable for off-road vehicles which could be used to shorten the distance. There are numerous places along the route where you can stop in case of emergency. From Rifugio Biella you descend by the track or, better still, by the bridle path (trail sign 6) to the summer pastures of the vast and lush Alpe di Sennes with Rifugio Sennes (2,126 m/6,973 ft; 1 hour; 41 beds; tel. (0)474/51092). From here proceed along the military road across Pian de Lasta, past the mountain houses of Fodara Vedla (1,980 m/6,494 ft; refuge) and finally, round many hairpin bends, to the Albergo di Pederü where, at the head of Val Tamersc' (Tamores), actually in the Sennes-Fanes Nature Reserve, you reach the scenic paved road from Marebbe (path 7; 1,540 m/5,051 ft; 2–3 hours).

The hotel has 23 beds (tel. (0)474/51086) and offers

SAUSSURITES OR DOLOMITES?

In 1788 Deodat de Gratet, a French nobleman better known as Dolomieu (after the castle where he was born), and professor of mineralogy at the Paris Museum, discovered, in the course of a trip in the outskirts of Bolzano, a mineral which looked like calcite. Unlike the latter, however, when it came into contact with muriatic acid it gave off only very slight effervescence.

His curiosity aroused, he sent off a sample to his colleague Théodore de Saussure, son of the famous Geneva scientist, Horace Benedicte de Saussure. Théodore found that the sample differed from ordinary limestone, being a double compound of carbonate and magnesium. In honour of the father, Dolomieu proposed calling it "Saussurite," but Théodore refused; subsequently researchers decided to name it after its accidental discoverer – "Dolomite." The term came to be used beyond the realms of science. In the nineteenth century, in fact, English mountaineers exploring the southern Tyrol and Trentino gave the name to the mountains they were preparing to climb. And so the "Pale Mountains" remained indissolubly linked with the name of Dolomieu, who never had the opportunity to visit them but is still considered to be the true scientific discoverer today.

On pages 146 and 147: a splendid view of the Averau group, imposing mountains which often assume a dark and menacing appearance.

One of the majestic panoramas in the Dolomites to be enjoyed on walks through this mountain region of entrancing beauty.

transport to the Alpe di Fanes Piccola (Munt de Pices Fanes; Kleine Fanesalpe). On foot, the road up to the Val di Rudo takes about 1½ hours. At the alp, a large karst basin is bounded on the west by the slopes of Sasso della Croce and Sasso delle Dieci, and guests are welcome at the two privately owned refuges: Rifugio Fanes (2,060 m/6,757 ft; 55 beds; tel. (0)474/51097) and Rifugio La Varella (2,038 m/6,684 ft; 40 beds; tel. (0)474/51079).

Detour: From Fodera Alta you can follow the high path which joins the road to the Alpe di Fanes at Lago Piciodel without the need to come down to Pederü.

Rifugio Fanes to Rifugio Dibona   H

19 km (11¾ miles), 6¾ hours, change in elevation 1,245 m (4,083 ft) uphill, 805 m (2,640 ft) downhill

A very varied stage, more strenuous because of the length than the changes in elevation, but with many scenic features (the rock faces of Cima Scotoni, Tofana) and points of historic interest (remnants of the First World War). The basic itinerary, described here, is the easiest to negotiate but there are many

variants, including *Vie Ferrate*, the climbing routes reserved for the experienced and fit hiker carrying suitable equipment.

From Rifugio Fanes take the military road and climb to Passo Limo (2,170 m/7,117 ft; small lake), around the head of the Val di Fanes (turning on left for Cortina d'Ampezzo) and continue south to Passo Tadega (2,157 m/7,075 ft). Beyond this take the bridle path through a broad corridor covered with pastures between the Fanes and Cunturines groups and then to the brink of Col d'La Locia (2,069 m/6,786 ft). You now descend below Cima del Lago (path equipped with wire cable) until you reach the road that climbs from the Capanna Alpina to Rifugio Scotoni (1,985 m/6,511 ft; 2¾ hours; 15 beds).

From Rifugio Scotoni the bridle track (path 20) winds down to Lec da Lagaciò and then, among remnants of the First World War in the Lagazuoi valley, climbs to Forcella Lagazuoi (2,572 m/8,436 ft; 2 hours) between Grande Lagazuoi and Piccolo Lagazuoi (cableway arrival station of Passo Falzarego; Rifugio Lagazuoi reached in about ½ hour, 34 beds).

You can get to Forcella Lagazuoi (*forcella* = a

saddle) directly by climbing a steep path which branches off the main route just before Col d'La Locia and crosses Forcella del Lago (2,480 m/8,134 ft), without passing Rifugio Scotoni.

Now comes the third and final part of this long stage: crossing Forcella di Travenanzes (2,513 m/8,142 ft) and, beneath it, Forcella Col dei Bos to the foot of Castelletto delle Tofane (path 402; 2,330 m/7,642 ft), you reach the south wall of Tofana di Rozes. The path (sign 404) skirts all along the face, 850 m (2,788 ft) high, and eventually meets the cart track which descends to Rifugio Dibona (2,083 m/6,832 ft; 2 hours; 25 beds; tel. (0)346/60294).

Rifugio Dibona to Rifugio Città di Fiume   H

18 km (11 miles), 7 hours, change in elevation 890 m (2,919 ft) uphill, 1,150 m (3,772 ft) downhill

This may be regarded as another transfer stage. Leaving behind the Tofane group, you now head towards the no less splendid Pelmo peaks. The walk,

Below: the Rifugio VII Alpini (1,498 m/ 4,913 ft) in the Pis Pilon, overlooked by the south face of Schiara. The refuge is a halt for those choosing to tackle the arduous climb of Schiara.

THE HIGH-LEVEL WALKS OF THE DOLOMITES

The *Alta Via n. 1* is the first of a series of high-level walks which have been formulated since the 1960s to enable walkers to visit the most interesting parts of the Dolomites (the photograph shows Passo del Gotto on Monte Pelmo). Today there are six such *Alte Vie*, each with different characteristics to suit walkers of all levels of experience. The paths, extending from north to south, cover more than 1,000 km (620 miles).

The most westerly is no. 2, known also as the *"Alta Via delle Leggende"* ("Fairy-Tale Walk") because it runs through areas associated with Ladin legend. It begins at Bressanone and ends at Feltre, including on the way the famous Sella, Marmolada and Pale di San Martino mountain groups. The route is broken down into fourteen stages, some of which are quite difficult, and is therefore suitable only for experienced hikers.

The *Alta Via* no. 1 is described in these pages while no. 3 is known as the *"Alta Via dei Camosci"* ("Chamois Walk") because for some of the way it follows the old trails of hunters, on paths that link Villabassa in Val Pusteria with Longarone in the Valle del Piave.

The *Alte Vie* no.s 4 and 5, commemorating respectively the Viennese climber Paul Grohmann and the artist Titian (Tiziano Vecellio), depart from points fairly close to each other at San Candido and at Sesto in Val Pusteria. After encircling the Marmole group they come together, with their last four stages coinciding, leading to Pieve di Cadore. These itineraries both have stretches fitted with fixed ropes and ladders; no. 5 in particular requires fitness and some high-mountain experience.

The *Alta Via* no. 6 is the most remote and isolated route and is known as the *"Alta Via dei Silenzi"* ("Silence Walk"). Unlike the others, it flanks the Carnic and Belluno Prealps between the Veneto and Friuli Venezia Giulia regions, and links the sources of the Piave north of Sappada to Vittorio Veneto across wild and uninhabited mountain zones. The 160-km (100-mile) trip is broken down into nine stages.

Above: the crossroads for Rifugio Fanes and La Varella. An example of the detailed signposting that guides walkers in the Dolomites.

Below: the Venezia tower which stands at the southern tip of the huge wall of Civetta.

through woods and pastures, is very varied and never too strenuous. From the refuge you descend by the driveway track to the first bend where you take path 442 as far as the Dolomite Road (Cortina d'Ampezzo–Passo Falzarego) at Cianzopè (1,732 m/5,681 ft); cross it and climb the road on the opposite slope which leads to Rifugio Cinque Torri at the foot of Torre Grande di Averau (2,137 m/7,009 ft; 1¾ hours; 14 beds; tel. (0)436/2902). Come down on path 437 until you meet the Cortina–Pocol–Passo Giau road and continue through the wood along the hillside to the bridle path which goes up to Pocol; this leads to Rifugio Palmieri and its small lake (2,046 m/6,711 ft; 2¾ hours; 32 beds; tel. (0)436/2085). You now face the long but not difficult walk across meadows to Rifugio Città di Fiume; apart from a 200-m (655-ft) climb at the start, this is all on the level and slightly downhill. After passing underneath Croda del Lago, you come to the saddles of Col Dur (sign 434), Roan (436), Puina (467) and finally to Rifugio Città di Fiume (1,918 m/6,291 ft; 2½ hours; 40 beds; tel. (0)437/720268).

Rifugio Città di Fiume to Rifugio Coldai   H–E

19 km (11¾ miles), 7½ hours, change in elevation 1,030 m (3,378 ft) uphill, 940 m (3,083 ft) downhill

This stage is divided into two distinct sections. The first comprises the stretch from Rifugio Città di Fiume to Rifugio Venezia (7 km/4¼ miles; 3 hours; change in elevation 560 m/1,837 ft uphill and about the same downhill); and it includes the most marvellous sight of the trip around the gravelly cirque of Val d'Arcia, namely the view of the north wall of Monte Pelmo (Flaibani path; three fixed safety ropes; take care if ground is icy). Rifugio Venezia, at the foot of the eastern wall of the Pelmo, has 74 beds (tel. (0)436/9684). The second section is longer (12 km/7½ miles) but with fewer changes in height (475 m/1,558 ft uphill, 380 m/1,246 ft downhill) and for the most part is over easy military roads.

From Rifugio Venezia you climb to the nearby Sella di Rutorto; then the path continues in a succession of ups and downs alongside the southern walls of Pelmo and Pelmetto, eventually meeting the paved

PARKS AND PROTECTED AREAS

In its first section, from the Lago di Braies to Lagazuoi (stages 1, 2 and 3), the High-Level Walk no. 1 runs through the Parco Naturale Fanes-Sennes-Braies. This park comprises an area of 25,680 hectares (63,430 acres) and protects a wide variety of plant and animal species. Among the former are rare dwarf orchids, and among the latter chamois, marmots, alpine hares and eagle owls.

In the final three stages the itinerary goes through the new Parco Nazionale delle Dolomiti Feltrine e Bellunesi which is being extended over some 30,000 hectares (74,100 acres) in the province of Belluno. It contains, among other features, the Schiara group but is noted in particular for the absence of large built-up areas: a zone of absolute wilderness, it is ideal for walkers.

road that links Zoldo Alto to Selva di Cadore at Forcella Staulanza (1,776 m/5,825 ft; privately owned refuge). Come down southward (Valle di Zoldo) to the first hairpin and take the road on the right for Casera Fontana Fredda. After just over 1 km, leave the road and take the left-hand path which climbs to Malga Vescovà (*malga* = summer pasture) (1,772 m/5,812 ft). The path now crosses Col dei Baldi (1,925 m/6,314 ft; skilifts) and descends to Forcella d'Alleghe (1,816 m/5,956 ft; refreshments). You then take the military road from Palafavera which winds upward to Rifugio Coldai (2,132 m/6,993 ft; 80 beds; tel. (0)437/789.160).

After a suitable rest it is worth pushing on to the nearby Forcella del Lago di Coldai (2,190 m/ 7,183 ft) to enjoy the sunset over Torre Coldai, Torre d'Alleghe and, above all, Civetta (¼ hour).

Rifugio Coldai to Rifugio Vazzoler   R

10.5 km (6½ miles), 3½ hours, change in elevation 130 m (426 ft) uphill, 560 m (1,837 ft) downhill

The north-western face of Civetta, described as "the wall of walls," extends horizontally for 7 km (4¼ miles) and stands over 1,200 m (3,936 ft) high. With its rows of towers and spires it has been likened to a gigantic pipe organ.

This is the most rewarding stretch of the *Alta Via*. The route is almost entirely on the flat, along path 560 which joins Forcella Coldai and the ensuing Forcella del Col Negro (2,203 m/7,226 ft) to the saddle of Col di Pelsa (1,954 m/6,409 ft). You have to take a diversion on the right which brings you in about half an hour to Rifugio Tissi (2,262 m/7,419 ft; 47 beds; tel. (0)437/72164) and the adjacent Col Rean (2,281 m/7,481 ft). This provides the most spectacular view of Civetta, opposite, but the panorama also takes in the south wall of the Marmolada, Sella, the mountains of the Val Badia and the Pale di San Martino.

From Col di Pelsa you begin the descent, first on the path and then, near the Casera Favretti (1,827 m/5,992 ft), by the jeep road which leads to the Rifugio Vazzoler (1,714 m/5,662 ft; 75 beds; tel. (0)437/62163). You are now at the southern end of the huge rock face of Civetta which rises still higher with the splendid walls of Torre Venezia and Torre Trieste.

MOUNTAINS BORN OUT OF THE SEA

The fossils which can still be found in the rocks of the Dolomites testify to the origins of these extraordinary mountains. They go back 200 million years when the whole area was covered by a huge, shallow sea and warm waters, with an abundance of lagoons, barrier reefs and coral islands. Over a period of 30 million years the organisms which inhabited this ocean (calcareous algae, molluscs, foraminiferans, corals, sponges, etc.) deposited their remains on the bottom, becoming transformed into calcareous rock, while submarine eruptions poured streams of lava over the rocks and among the coral reefs.

In the following era, about 60 million years ago, the powerful thrust of the African land mass against the Eurasian land mass led to the emergence of those marine depths which were then transformed into gigantic mountains. At this point the work of atmospheric agents began: rain, wind, frost and thaw gradually broke down these structures, eroding them in different ways according to the composition of the rocks and the strata. The rock fragments derived from this disintegration tumbled to the foot of the mountains, forming characteristic slips of scree.

It was the excavating action of glaciers which added the finishing touch, cutting out and shaping the valleys with their surrounding sheer, stark rock walls. This process led to the fantastic mountain landscape of today: towers, spires and pinnacles mingling with more modestly flattened peaks, high plateaus and grassy saddles overlooked by precipitous rock walls and ledges.

Opposite: a view of Lago d'Alleghe which gives some idea of the incredible sights to be enjoyed along this high-level walk through the Dolomites.

Rifugio Vazzoler to Rifugio Carestiato   H

8 km (5 miles), 4½ hours, change in elevation
540 m (1,771 ft) uphill, 400 m (1,312 ft) downhill

This stage represents the most southerly sector of the
Alta Via. This is a wilder and far less populated area,
and for this reason has been designated as the setting
of the Parco Nazionale delle Dolomiti Bellunesi.

The paths here are less distinct and not as well
signposted as the previous ones, and the *rifugi* are
fewer and further apart.

From Rifugio Vazzoler you follow the access road
of the Val Corpassa which initially passes under
Torre Venezia and then descends in sharp turns. At
the crossroads (1,420 m/4,657 ft) you leave it (restock
water supply at the stream) and turn left for a long
trek which takes you completely around the Moiazza
group, first via the western slopes past the Forcella
del Col Palanzin and Forcella del Col dell'Ors (narrow ledge protected by metal cables) and eventually,
after Forcella di Casera del Camp, along the southern side. Rifugio Carestiato stands on the wooded
slope of the Col di Pass, at the foot of the Pala di
Belia, from which there is a fine view (1,834 m/6,015
ft; 35 beds; tel. (0)437/62942).

Rifugio Carestiato to Rifugio Sommariva   H

8 km (5 miles), 4½ hours, change in elevation
540 m (1,771 ft) uphill, 400 m (1,312 ft) downhill

From Rifugio Carestiato come down along the access
road of Passo Duran (1,611 m/5,284 ft) on to the road
linking Agordo with the Valle di Zoldo (Rifugio
Tomè and Rifugio Albergo San Sebastiano). From
the pass you have to follow the road on the Agordo
side for about 2 km (1¼ miles) as far as the Casera di
Calleda bend. Here the most interesting part of this
stage begins, running past the western slopes of the
Tamer group and of the Moschesin from the Forcella
Dagarei (1,620 m/5,313 ft) to the Forcella Moschesin
(1,940 m/6,363 ft), across grassy hillsides, scree slips
and clumps of mugo pines.

From Forcella Moschesin, after a brief descent,
you head east past the top of the Val di Pramper to
the huge grassy bowl of Prà della Vedova and Rifugio
Sommariva al Pramperet (1,857 m/6,091 ft; 40 beds;
tel. (0)437/78214).

On pages 158 and 159: a close-up of the Cinque Torre d'Averau; its resemblance to a giant natural castle makes it one of the most popular rock-climbing areas of the Dolomites.

Below: Lago Coldai (2190 m/7,183 ft), not far from the col of that name (2,191 m/7,186 ft), from which there is a view of the Marmolada and the first towers of the north crest of Civetta.

Rifugio Sommariva to Rifugio Bianchet   H

10 km (6¼ miles), 6 hours, change in elevation 800 m (2,624 ft) uphill, 765 m (2,509 ft) downhill

This is the easiest part of the route and recommended for walkers without alpine experience. The way down to Belluno via Rifugio Bianchet in fact avoids crossing Schiara and the long descent of its southern face, this being one of the most arduous stretches of the *Alta Via* (*Via Ferrata* [climbing route]: diff. EE).

From the refuge you ascend to Portela del Piazedel, crossing the gravelly cirque and then areas of rock, detritus and hummocks of grass to Forcella Sud del Vant de Zità (2,395 m/7,855 ft) from where you can admire Schiara. You now descend the detritus-strewn basin of the Vant de Zità de Fora; at the bottom a path (sign 514) twists and turns down to the dal Mas mountain hut below (1,632 m/5,353 ft; 3 hours; 5 km/3 miles; 15 bunks).

From the hut continue down along path 514 to a crossroads; instead of taking the left turn which descends into the Valle dei Rossi (Longarone), branch right for the zigzag climb to Forcella La-

varetta (1,074 m/3,552 ft) which is situated between Schiara and its Talvena subgroup.

You now proceed south-east towards Schiara along a scenic route which climbs from the head of the Val Vescovà to the crossroads before Casonet di Nerville. Path 514 brings you face to face with Schiara (Marmol hut and Rifugio del VII Alpini; diff. E) but our route bears right (sign 518) and zigzags down to the bottom of the Val Vescovà where, in the middle of the Pian dei Gat, you arrive at Rifugio Bianchet (1,245 m/4,083 ft; 40 beds; tel. 0437/87294).

Rifugio Bianchet to Belluno   R

13 km (8 miles), 2 hours, change in elevation 760 m (2,493 ft) downhill

The High-Level Walk is now almost at an end. All that is left is to descend the forest road that is the driveway to the refuge until you reach the paved road of the Val Cordevole; follow this for about 1 km to the village of La Muda (483 m/1,584 ft; bus stop for Belluno).

Above: Rifugio Venezia de Luca, at the foot of the east wall of Pelmo, reached during the seventh stage of the Walk.

FRANCE

CORSICAN HIGH-LEVEL ROUTE

Grande Randonnée 20

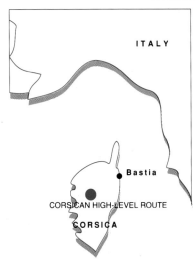

ITALY

Bastia

CORSICAN HIGH-LEVEL ROUTE

CORSICA

Useful addresses: Parc Naturel Régional de la Corse, BP 417 – 20184 Ajaccio Cedex – tel. 95-215654.
Maps: Maps, 1:50,000, Corse Nord – de Calvi à Vizzavona and Corse Sud – de Vizzavona à la Montagne de Cagna of the Institut Géographique National.
Bibliography: A. Castle, *The Corsican High-Level Route*, Cicerone Press, Cumbria; R. G. Collomb, *Corsican Mountains*, West Col Productions, Reading; or the French "GR 20, Topo Guide des sentiers de Grande Randonnée."

The Corsican High-Level Route is one of the French *Grande Randonnée* walks and is known as GR 20. The route traces the natural features and cultural highlights of the Corsican hinterland and lies within Le Parc Naturel Régional de la Corse. It runs from north-west to south-east along the watershed forming the backbone of the island, linking the villages of Calenzana and Conca. This itinerary through mountainous terrain provides an opportunity to appreciate the ancient traditions of pastoral life amid wild, contrasting scenery which, with its waterfalls and age-old forests, includes stretches similar to that of the great parks of North America. The entire route, over bridle tracks and mountain paths, covers a distance of about 180 km (112 miles) and is regarded as a classic itinerary, one of the most challenging in Europe. Such a reputation is in part justified by the fact that walkers have to be virtually self-sufficient in terms of food and other supplies and that they must be prepared to encounter abrupt changes in elevation over rough, uneven terrain.

In the northern section the lie of the land gives rise to splendid scenery that is reminiscent of the Alps. The massifs of Monte Cinto, 2,710 m (8,890 ft) and Monte Rotondo, 2,622 m (8,600 ft) are covered in snow until late spring, being situated in the center of the island yet only a few miles from the sea. The

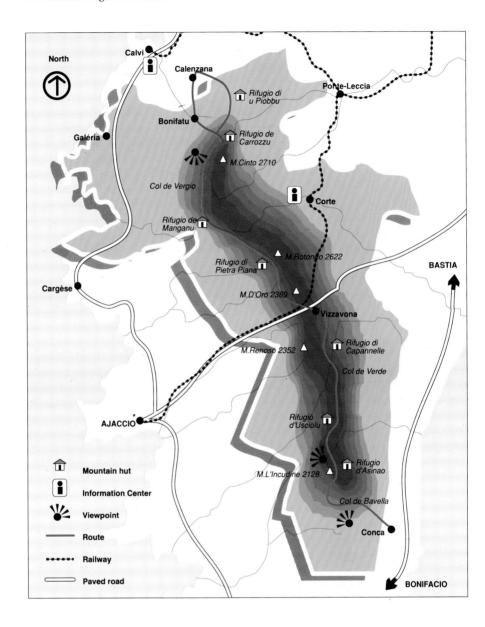

Distance: 180 km (112 miles), divided into 14/15 stages.

Departure point: Conca, immediately inland; accessible by taxi from Santa Lucia di Porto Vecchio, on the Basta–Porto Vecchio bus route.

Arrival point: Calenzana, linked with Calvi on the coast by local bus service (daily, except Sundays and national holidays); from Calvi, ferries to the mainland or train to Bastia.

Where to stay: Good mountain huts along route but no stocking-up possibilities.

Signposting: White and red signs with mountain routes; valley connections normally marked in yellow on tree trunks or on rocks.

Difficulty: E – Expert walkers: the length of the journey, the changes in elevation, some exposed stretches requiring the support of fixed ropes, and self-sufficiency in food make the GR 20 a demanding itinerary.

When to go: June and September are the best months.

Equipment: Mid-mountain to high altitude; a tent is not essential, and surviving without one will lighten the amount to be carried.

southern part which slopes gradually down to the coast, on the other hand, demands less expenditure of energy and is more under the influence of the Mediterranean climate.

This substantial difference makes it possible to divide the whole journey into two distinct parts which come together at Vizzavona, in the middle of the island. It also means that, when deciding in what month to go, bear in mind that the southern section is at its best in the autumn when the woods are alive with colour, while early summer offers the ideal climatic conditions for the northern stretch.

The Corsicans

The visitor to Corsica will notice how the majority of the island's seaside resorts are owned and run by French immigrants. It is understandable, therefore, that the Corsican people, still searching even today for their own identity, are somewhat wary of anyone coming to their island from overseas.

Withdrawn and introverted, with a quiet dignity, the Corsicans are instinctively mountain people of the interior rather than seagoing folk of the coast. Visitors will notice them mostly commuting by train from one side of the island to the other or living in the hill villages of the hinterland where their sometimes wretched condition is the result of a population exodus that still continues. Recently, however, a reversal of this trend has been noticeable, whereby the native Corsicans have begun to rediscover their island, their culture and their folklore. Because most native Corsicans live inland, this is where the local dialect is most commonly heard. Although it may not be easy to enter into serious conversation with the inhabitants, knowledge of Italian or French does at least provide a point of contact.

Our Corsican itinerary starts at the coast and climbs up into the wooded valleys of the immediate hinterland. Beyond the villages, built for defence reasons on mountain ridges where one slope was likely to be inaccessible, the bridle tracks leading to the upper pastures lead to the GR 20 where nature is wild and signs of human presence few and far between. From here you get only distant glimpses of the villages down in the valley and the few people you chance to meet will be the shepherds who live temporarily on the summer pastures in stone and wood

USEFUL ADVICE

Provisions: As the route is mainly along mountain ridges, the chances of buying provisions on the GR 20 are virtually nil, simply because there are so few people living thereabouts. Walkers can either try to buy local produce, not always available for sale, in the *bergeries* along the route, or restock at any of the places along the GR 20 which lie on a road (Conca, Col di Bavella, Capannelle, Vizzavona, Castel de Verghio, Calenzana). There are also plenty of paths linking places and, in case of emergency, there is invariably a quick way down to the bottom of the valley. Only on a few stages of the itinerary is it possible to obtain fresh water and in midsummer such opportunities are only to be found at high altitude.

Climate: As is often the case in mountains, the weather is generally best early in the morning, but may well change for the worse unexpectedly. The wind can be a nuisance, while mist, suddenly sweeping down into a rocky gorge, may pose orientation problems which should not be underestimated. Early summer is, by and large, the best time to embark on the trek, but for those wishing to divide the trip into two, late September is ideal for the autumn coloration of the beech woods along the southern stretch.

The route: French guide books generally describe the route from north to south. However, since this is purely a matter of choice, we have opted here for the opposite direction with a view to offering walkers an itinerary which becomes more spectacular and challenging as it goes.

In a country where there are all too many signs of the damage done to woods and forests by fires, generally caused by carelessness, it is important to emphasize the risk of sparking off a blaze in the extremely dry undergrowth. And, as always, walkers are urged not to leave refuse anywhere along the route.

On pages 166 and 167: from Col di Bavella you can interrupt the trek and go down to the coast on the Solenzana road.

mountain pasture huts, called *bergeries*. These may provide an opportunity to buy a few local dairy products if the shepherds are willing to do trade with the occasional passing tourists.

Flora and fauna

Unlike the nearby island of Sardinia, which has uniform mountainous surroundings all over without widespread tree cover, the Corsican hinterland is full of surprises and unexpected contrasts. Whereas the higher western block rises sheer above the sea and is made up chiefly of crystalline rock, the eastern, partially of the schist type, tends to decline gradually, forming an alluvial coastline.

The GR 20 is a high-level walk with views over mountains and valley villages, sometimes reaching the coastline on the horizon.

The varied and spectacular landscape is impressive and awe-inspiring. Below is a luxuriant tangle of Mediterranean maquis, with powerfully scented plant species, and higher up in the mountains are great forests of conifers where the Corsican pine (also known as the Corsican fir or larch), the

island's symbol, grows in solitary majesty on the crags.

The coastal vegetation of agave, cactus and eucalyptus gives way to hills, vineyards, orchards and cork woods, while inland broadleaved trees include chestnut, ilex and beech.

The fauna of the interior, once prolific, has in recent years been subjected to severe hunting pressure. The animals most frequently encountered are to be found in the high pastures, notably the wild boar which comes out at dusk in search of food. Among the granite pinnacles of the Col di Bavella, a trained eye may be able to spot the rare mouflon, now decimated by continuous poaching over the years.

In late spring countless streams pour down from the mountains through zones of luxuriant vegetation; but despite this quantity of water, frequent fires, often caused by arson, put the delicate ecological balance of the Corsican island under ever increasing threat.

LE PARC NATUREL RÉGIONAL DE LA CORSE

The Corsican Regional Nature Park, established in 1972, covers an area roughly one fifth of the island's total, consisting of lengthy stretches of northern and western coastlines together with a series of mountain massifs that form the backbone of Corsica.

The purpose of instituting such a park was not merely to conserve the environment but also to preserve those forms of local tradition which were slowly disappearing as a result of the gradual depopulation of the hinterland. The jobs created to provide forest rangers and management for mountain huts, plus the opportunity for local people to make a profit from shops opened for hikers, have partly checked the population exodus without affecting the delicate equilibrium of the region.

The itinerary

More than 180 km (112 miles) of paths and tracks, a total change in elevation of 10,150 m (33,300 ft) uphill and 10,100 m (33,130 ft) downhill, and an estimated minimum period of 14 days (six for the southern tract and eight for the northern), with the possibility of prolonging the holiday by taking some of the signposted scenic detours: these are the essential details of the GR 20 that a walker will need on leaving the coast for the hinterland of Corsica, intent on discovering the delights of this fascinating island.

Conca to Rifugio Paliri　　　　　　　H

12 km (7½ miles), 6½ hours, change in elevation 1,050 m (3,445 ft) uphill, 200 m (656 ft) downhill

From the village (252 m/826 ft) you climb through the maquis to the Bocca d'Usciolu (587 m/1,925 ft; 1¼ hours). The route heads inland in a north-west direction along the barren, dry hillside where there are clear traces of past fires.

The path continues up and down, twice crossing the Rio di Punta Pizzuta, a stream with water clear and deep enough to bathe in on hot days.

Proceeding through scrubland and pine woods,

The suspension bridge over the Anglai Falls, one hour's walk from Vizzavona.

WILD PIGS AND WILD BOARS

In the Vizzavona forest, on Col di Bavella and in the tangled Mediterranean maquis, there is a large population of wild boars. It is not uncommon for those pigs (photograph below) which graze untended to mate with the boars, thus increasing the number of wild pigs that cannot be easily distinguished from true boars.

Hikers need to be warned that such animals may become aggressive if they smell food at a camping site. Take care never to leave tents or rucksacks containing food unattended. Anyone who has been trekking in North America will be aware of the procedure of packing and storing provisions in trees to protect them from the ravages of bears. Although the situation is somewhat different, the same principle applies here.

you climb to the remains of the summer pasture of Capello (850 m/2,788 ft; 2½ hours; spring 100 m/ 300 ft north). The GR 20 now leads to the top of a plateau, the Breche de Villaghello, with unusual formations caused by wind erosion (1,040 m/3,411 ft). You descend a steep gorge to the Foce di u Bracciu (905 m/2,968 ft) and then climb again to the col of Mt Bracciuto, in a beautiful setting of pines and dense scrub, overlooked by towering rock walls.

The last stretch, still uphill, leads through a young pine plantation to the demolished *bergerie* of Paliri, where the small Paliri refuge (1,080 m/3,542 ft) stands below the south-eastern slope of Punta Tafonata.

Rifugio Paliri to Rifugio d'Asinao   H

15 km (9¼ miles), 7 hours, change in elevation 650 m (2,132 ft) uphill, 310 m (1,016 ft) downhill

After a stretch along the hillside, the path climbs to the Foce Finosa (1,206 m/3,955 ft; ¾ hour), enclosing the southern buttresses of the Punta Tafonata di i Paliri, where the effect of erosion has shaped the rock into fantastic and bizarre forms.

There is a fine view of the opposite slope and the Bavella forest; on the descent you soon come to a narrow forest road, crossing the Rio San Petrus, and then branch off through the wood for the Col di Bavella (1,218 m/3,995 ft; 1¼ hours). The tinkling bells of young goats at pasture herald your arrival, after a short climb, at the summer village of Bavella (possibility of refreshments and accommodation). From the D 1268 road you now follow the winding, narrow path which descends to sea level at Solenzara through the vast state forest that looks down on the granite amphitheater where mouflon live and various birds of prey nest. From the col, on which grow some splendid Corsican pines, the GR 20 descends to the south-west and then along the hillside, eventually making a long, twisting semi-circle around the mountains of Bavella and the Corni d'Asinao. Beyond the crest of the Pargulu, the route enters the valley of the Asinao river and an easy climb leads you, in just under five hours from Bavella, to the summer pasture and refuge of Asinao (1,530 m/5,018 ft), situated high on the right of the river, on the slopes of Mt Incudine.

Detour – Ridge route: from the Col di Bavella

there is a mountain-climbing detour which crosses the three Torri d'Asinao, with exposed stretches (fixed ropes) but inadvisable if weather conditions (mist and wind) are bad.

Rifugio D'Asinao to Rifugio d'Usciolu   E

17 km (10½ miles), change in elevation 1,000 m (3,210 ft) uphill, 800 m (2,624 ft) downhill

Since the Rifugio Pedinielli was destroyed by fire in 1984 this has become one of the longest stages of the entire GR 20: if you take a tent, you can camp near Pedinielli and break the itinerary down into two shorter stages.

From the refuge the track leads first north-west and then, along the line of the crest, north-east; the hard climb brings you to the summit of Mt Incudine (2,134 m/7,000 ft; 2½ hours). The final stretch of the descent is along grassy slopes westward to the remains of Rifugio Pedinielli (1,623 m/5,323 ft; 1¼ hours). The path enters the beech wood and there is a

The GR 20 ends on the north-west coast which, with its hidden coves, often inaccessible by land, forms part of the Parc Natural Régional de la Corse.

suspension bridge over the Casmintellu stream. Whereas the Incudine landscape was stark, the scenery is now richer, with splendid beech woods and the smooth, undulating expanse of the Coscione plateau, in a region modelled by glacial erosion.

Climbing through the woods, you reach Bocca d'Agnone (1,570 m/5,150 ft; 3 hours) and then follow, in a north-east direction beyond the treeline, the watershed along the ridge, this region being known as Arête des Statues. On clear days you can see both the east and west coasts of the island. The long journey is now almost over, and the path leads down

The lush landscape of fields and meadows around Lake Nino is in some ways reminiscent of the Far North and testifies to the scenic variety of the Corsican interior.

to Rifugio d'Usciolu (1,750 m/5,740 ft), on the slopes of Mt Formicola.

Detour – There are many paths that lead down into the valley, the most important of which are those to the villages of Zicavo and Cozzano.

Rifugio d'Usciolu to Rifugio de Prati   H

12 km (7½ miles), change in elevation 680 m (2,230 ft) uphill, 600 m (1,968 ft) downhill

The GR 20 ascends (1½ hours) to the vast rocky plain of Col du Brouillard (1,950 m/6,396 ft), on the

GLOSSARY

Some everyday Corsican vocabulary:

Rural activities and tools

basket, bag	cuffa, curbella
olive pickers	cugliatori
clearing the undergrowth	diraschera
olive crusher	fragnu
daily route of flocks	invistita
sheaf	manna
hoe	marascutu
harvest	sighera
seller of oil	trangulinu
countryman	zappaghjolu

Plants and fruits

chestnut husk	bogula
roast chestnuts	fasgiole
chestnut	nuccella, villana
strawberry tree	albitru
olive	alivu
fir	fagu
lentisk	lustincu
myrtle	mortula
heather	scopa

Parts of the home

stone wash-basin	acquagnu
staircase	balltoghju
lightning conductor	calamita
cellar	carciula
cheese-making area	casgile
lavatory	cacatoghju
balcony	cacciafora
sheep pen	chjostra
hearth	fucone
woodshed	lignaghju
window	purtellu
sheepfold	stazzu

Domestic furnishings and utensils

chair	carreca
coffee-pot	chiccara
frying-pan	frissoghja
oil lamp	lampera
stool	pedinu
crockery	piattera
table	tola
apron	sculzale

Clothing

dark velvet beret	barretta pinzuta
shirt	camisgià
man's short coat	caputtu
handkerchief	mezzaru

eastern side of Mt Formicola. It then leads down to the beech woods and to Col de Laparo, a main crossroads with route to the bottom of the valley (1,525 m/5,002 ft; 1½ hours), continuing by way of the ridge along the western side of Punta Campolongo. The terrain, at first easy (Col de Rapari; 1,614 m/5,294 ft), later becomes rough: where the path disappears as it crosses stony ground, the itinerary becomes something of a hit and miss affair as you follow the line of the watershed from one ridge to the next. Once over the spurs of Punta Cappella (2,000 m/6,560 ft) and a brief level stretch, you descend to the broad grassy platform where Rifugio de Prati (1,840 m/6,035 ft) stands in a dominating position above the eastern plain and the sea. On clear days it is possible to see the island of Monte Cristo on the horizon.

Remember: during this whole stage there is no chance of restocking with water; it is therefore necessary to take advantage of the stop at the Rifugio d'Usciolu to fill up with as much water as you need.

Detours – At Col de Laparo there are paths connecting with the valley bottom: eastward to the village of San Gavino, westward to Col de Verde following the detour of the old track of the GR 20 which runs through the forest of Piattone, avoiding the ridge and the climb to Rifugio de Prati.

Rifugio de Prati to Rifugio di Capannelle   H

16 km (10 miles), 6 hours, change in elevation 590 m (1,935 ft) uphill, 820 m (2,690 ft) downhill

This stage, on a slight gradient as far as Col de Prati, bears north-west and then descends to Col de Verde (1,289 m/4,228 ft; 1½ hours), through beech then conifer woods.

The GR 20 crosses the D 69 secondary road close to the col refuge and climbs the valley of Rio Taravo on a forest road as far as Col de la Flasca (1,430 m/4,690 ft; ¾ hour). On the opposite side you descend to the valley of Rio Marmano through a forest of conifers which include some gigantic firs. After fording that stream, you climb a steep path up to the open meadows of Piana di Gialgone (1,591 m/5,218 ft; 1 hour). The next part has no steep stretches but the scenery, dominated by beech woods, is quite wonderful, the trees displaying a fantastic range of tints, particularly in autumn.

After reaching the road leading to Capannelle, you climb past the Traghette summer pastures to Rifugio di Capannelle (1,590 m/5,215 ft), near the ski resort.

Detour – Ascent of Mt Renoso (2,352 m/7,714 ft): the track departs from Capannelle and rejoins the GR 20 on the Gialgone plateau.

The beech wood (photograph above) tinged with autumnal colours; the fallen leaves almost completely conceal the pools formed by the torrents which pour down from the mountain (photograph below).

Rifugio di Capannelle to Vizzavona   H

13 km (8 miles), 4½ hours, change in elevation 200 m (656 ft) uphill, 800 m (2,624 ft) downhill

The route descends rapidly to Sambuco: there are no particular difficulties to be encountered along this stage and the stretch linking the Scarpaccedie summer pastures to those of Alzeta is through beautiful woodland. A winding but easy bridle track follows the line of several hilly ridges, the upper slopes of which are covered with beech and those lower down, towards the valley, with conifers. Many brooks and streams cross the track.

Heading north, you continue climbing, past the treeline, as far as Bocca Palmente (1,640 m/5,379 ft; 2¾ hours from Capannelle). From here you descend to Vizzavona (920 m/3,017 ft; 1½ hours), emerging from the woodland of twisted beech, where the high ground lacks humus and provides little plant nutrition, into the majestic conifer forest of Vizzavona.

NORTH-WEST COAST

Features: Part of the Parc Naturel Régional de la Corse on the stretch of coast between Calvi and Porto is made up of the final spur of the island's highest mountains. The steep walls overhanging the sea, predominantly crystalline in formation, prevent access from land to the many rocky coves. Walkers ending their journey at Calenzana can experience the added challenge of trying to find a way along twisting paths or mule tracks to some of the most unspoiled and beautiful parts of the Corsican coast.

Access: As the crow flies, it is not far from Calvi to Porto but the D 81 road linking the two towns is long and winding. To reach the cliffs it is necessary to leave the road and hunt for the track that leads down through the scrubland to the sea (Golfo della Girolata); on the other hand, where the terrain is not so rugged and more open, it is easier to get down to the beach (Baia di Galeria).

SOUTH-EAST COAST

Features: The stretch of coastline that runs from Porto Vecchio down to Bonifacio, the southern tip of the island, is not as remote as the north-western tract. Because of its relative accessibility, there are more seaside tourist resorts. Even so, some of the loveliest and most noted beaches and bays are to some extent still quite wild and un-spoiled, especially if you manage to go out of season. Among these are: north of Porto Vec-chio, the beach of Cavu, on the estuary of the Cavu river; between Porto Vecchio and Bonifacio Palombaggia (photograph below), the bay of Santa Giulia, Cala Rondinara, the gulf of Santa Manza, and the beaches of Cala Longa and Pian-tarella facing the islands of Cavallo and Lavezzi.

Access: From the east coast road which links Porto Vecchio and Bonifacio, there are many roads branching off to the loveliest beaches. Those that are dirt tracks rather than paved lead to the less crowded spots.

INLAND: CORTE

Features: In the center of the island, at the con-fluence of the Tavignano and the Restonica, is Corte (417 m/1,367 ft), historical capital of Cor-sica and focus of the nationalist movement for Corsican independence. The old fortified citadel is situated high on the rocks and merits a visit. The walks up the Tavignano and Restonica valleys to the GR 20 are also interesting.

Access: Corte is linked with the coast by the Bastia–Ajaccio railway line and road which both run diagonally across the island from north-east to south-west. For those who want to visit the town, Corte can be reached by train from Vizzavona which is on the GR 20 route.

This is the undisputed realm of the wild boar which often mates with domesticated wild pigs. Having reached the road, you can spend the night at the Forestale camping site or in one of the hotels or the station inn at Vizzavona, on the only railway line that links the center of the island with the coast. This is the end of the southern tract of the GR 20; so if you are combining the two sections of the itinerary, stock up with provisions.

Vizzavona to Rifugio de l'Onda   H

9.5 km (6 miles), 6 hours, change in elevation 1,130 m (3,706 ft) uphill, 670 m (2,197 ft) downhill

Leaving the Forestale di Vizzavona camping site, you head south-west on a dirt road and, after less than an hour's walk through the wood, reach the picturesque waterfalls, Les Cascades des Anglais (1,150 m/3,772 ft). Crossing the bridge over the Agnone stream, you walk a short way up the right-hand mountain side, along a series of step faults with intermittent clear rock pools where it is tempting to stop.

The GR 20 now points directly north, making a broad semi-circle through the wood around the south-west slope of Mt d'Oro where, as you go higher, trees give way to shrubs. The climb up to the saddle, over rocky and stony terrain, is tiring but not difficult; once on the ridge, you head sharply west to the Muratello pass (2,064 m/6,770 ft; 3½ hours). Then you come down along an undulating ridge until you see the stone buildings that make up the Onda *bergeries* and, a little higher up, on the east slope of the hill, the small refuge (warden not always present) which marks the end of this first stage (1,430 m/ 4,690 ft).

Detour – Ascent of Mt D'Oro (2,389 m/7,836 ft): from Vizzavona you can reach the summit of Mt d'Oro, past the abandoned *bergeries* of Puzzatelli, on a track marked by a regular succession of stone mounds, later joining the GR 20 on the Muratello ridge.

Rifugio d'Onda to Rifugio de Pietra Piana   H

10 km (6¼ miles), 5½ hours, change in elevation 910 m (2,985 ft) uphill, 470 m (1,541 ft) downhill

Descend by a mule track through the woods of the Grottaccia valley to the confluence with the

PLACES TO STAY AND STOP ON THE GR 20

Because there are mountain huts on the Corsican High-Level Route, walkers do not need to carry a tent. During the summer (June to end-September), most of these huts offer reasonably complete facilities: between 15 to 30 beds with mattresses, lighting and gas-cooking area, and a fresh water tap just outside.

In the busiest periods, however, you may have to settle for camping in the open; there is a modest charge for an overnight stay in a refuge and for the use of the gas cooker for campers. If there is nobody in charge, you just slip the money into a box on the wall. Apart from the refuges along the route, here is a list of other refreshment and accommodation places with telephone.

Col di Bavella (1,218 m/3,995 ft): Two bar-restaurants with sleeping facilities in adjoining mountain huts.

Rifugio di Capannelle (1,640 m/5,379 ft): Near the refuge and the ski resort on the slopes of Mt Renoso is the "U Fugone" café-restaurant.

Vizzavona (920 m/3,017 ft): Near the station, open May/June to September: Hotel Beauséjour (tel. 95-472113); Hotel Réfuge de la Gare di Mme Tho (tel. 95-472119), accommodation in rooms with bunk beds and outside bathrooms; Hotel Restaurant Moderne (tel. 95-472112), hotel and refuge, more expensive but more comfortable.

Albergo Ristorante Castel de Verghio (1,330 m/4,362 ft): Tel. 95-480001, on the only road crossed by the GR 20 between Vizzavona and Calenzana.

Haut-Asco (1,422 m/4,664 ft): Hotel Restaurant Le Chalet (tel. 95-478108), hotel and refuge, departure point for Mt Cinto and now, after the Rifugio Altore fire, the destination for GR 20 hikers, with a detour to the valley from the standard ridge route.

Bonifato (540 m/1,771 ft): Restaurant and dormitory accommodation (tel. 95-650998), at the end of the D 251 road, near the Casa Forestale.

Manganello river (1¼ hours). Turning left, you cross the suspension bridge over cascades and natural pools, and soon come to the characteristic Bergerie de Tolla. The path leads gently upward into a forest of age-old pines, while to the left of the GR 20, in the wild and rugged landscape, the Manganello river presents foaming cascades, pools of icy water and the opportunity to have a quick, bracing swim. As you get higher, although the vegetation becomes ever more sparse and closer to the ground, its scent fills the air more and more. Occasional Corsican pines, solitary giants or white, petrified skeletons, lie up-rooted on the steep slopes of the valley, creating a natural landscape of overwhelming grandeur.

At the head of the valley the itinerary bears west and the path becomes decidedly steeper. You can stop among the ruins of the old summer pasture at Gialgo to catch your breath; then there is a final burst, round sharp bends, up to Rifugio di Pietra Piana (1,842 m/6,041 ft), perched on a grassy plateau alongside the mountain-rescue hut. This is the depar-ture point for the ascent of Mt Rotondo and is likely to be quite crowded, and not only in the months of July and August when it is more difficult to find anywhere to spend the night on the GR 20 unless you are carrying a tent.

Detour – Ridge route (5 hours): as an alternative to the valley route, which is longer but more varied and definitely advisable if the weather is bad, the ridge route detour links the two refuges on this stage, following the ridge in a north-west direction.

Rifugio de Pietra Piana to Rifugio Manganu   E

9.5 km (6 miles), 5¾ hours, change in elevation 550 m (1,804 ft) uphill, 790 m (2,591 ft) downhill

From the refuge, which you reach by climbing the hill ridge, the GR 20 continues north-west across stony ground along the hillside to Col de la Haute Route (2,206 m/7,235 ft; 1¼ hours), between the southern side of Maniccia and Punta Mozzello. Beyond, from the watershed, there are views of a truly extraordin-ary landscape of snowfields and glacial lakes, domi-nated by granitic towers and spires – quite astonishing for anyone accustomed to thinking of Corsica merely as a place of holiday seaside resorts.

There is now a gentle descent through easy snow-fields, which are still present in early summer, to Col

On pages 178 and 179: the surprising shapes taken on by certain plants reveal how they are constantly exposed to atmospheric agents.

de Rinoso (2,150 m/7,052 ft) above the lake of that name. The path leads down from the col towards Lake Melo, while higher up, tucked into the facing wall as if suspended, you can just get a glimpse of Lake Capitello. Bear left over stony terrain around the vast amphitheater and then climb once more along the line of the ridge to Bocca di Capitello (2,225 m/7,298 ft; 2½ hours). Although from a distance access to the pass appears difficult, if not impossible, you soon discover an easy trail leading through rocks and pinnacles rising sheer above Lake Capitello, but getting across any small snowfields that have not yet thawed by late June does need special care because of their steepness.

From the pass there is a long and sharp descent to the narrow valley of the Manganu river, but eventually it levels out into grassy plains, at which point Rifugio Manganu is already in sight (1,600 m/ 5,248 ft).

Detours – Ascent of Mt Rotondo (2,622 m/8,600 ft): the panoramic ascent of Mt Rotondo is one of the most popular challenges for experienced hikers in Corsica. The descent of the north slope brings you to

At Punta Tafonata di Ipalini the effects of erosion have carved bizarre shapes in the rock.

the Restonica valley and, by way of the road which climbs it, to the town of Corte.

– Lake Melo and Lake Capitello: from Bocca Soglia a path marked in yellow branches off the GR 20 to make a short detour to two of the most picturesque lakes of the hinterland route, rejoining it higher up near Punta alle Porte. North of Lake Melo another diversion leads to the head of the Restonica valley, starting point of the road to Corte.

Rifugio Manganu to Rifugio Ciottulu di I Mori   H

24.5 km (15¼ miles), 9 hours, change in elevation 1,030 m (3,378 ft) uphill, 620 m (2,033 ft) downhill

Given the time required and the length of the journey (approximately 6 hours and only 400 m/1,312 ft change in elevation), Castel de Verghio is a good place for an intermediate overnight stop.

From Manganu the GR 20 proceeds downhill: soon the valley opens up to form an undulating plain, the Pian di Campotile (1,540 m/5,051 ft). The track now continues to the north-west, past the Vaccaghia

Above: pools of crystal-clear water formed by the Agnone river invite walkers to paddle. Below: small snowfields, still present in late June, overlook Lake Rinoso which lies tucked among the rocks.

Two aspects of the Corsican landscape: above, shore vegetation in the Gulf of Galeria on the coast; below, Corsican pines on Col di Bavella, in the interior.

summer pasture (¾ hour) and into the Tavignano valley. Beyond the remains of an old mountain hut destroyed by fire, the walk is on the flat through woods, but as you climb the valley the soft, spongy undulations of the meadows are more similar to an Arctic tundra landscape. Continuing west, the route runs alongside Lake Nino, from which flows the Tavignano (1¾ hours) and climbs to Bocca a Reta (1,883 m/6,176 ft). Along the ridge and then downhill, the path crosses Col de S. Pierre (1,452 m/4,762 ft; 1¾ hours), from where you can glimpse the broad valley of the Valdo Niello forest and, in the distance, the Castel de Verghio skilifts. The path now winds down through the wood of beech and pine and then continues northward along the hillside for a considerable distance around the valley basin, eventually reaching the paved road which ascends to Col de Verghio, the highest pass negotiable by traffic on the island (1,464 m/4,802 ft).

If you want to round off the stage here, take the diversion, marked in yellow a little before, and climb through the wood to the hotel Castel de Verghio (1,404 m/4,605 ft).

In the village of Fer à Cheval, cross the road D 84 and enter the pine wood again. The valley becomes narrow and not far from the Radule falls, in a rugged, rocky landscape, you climb a gorge, passing the Radule summer pasture set among the crags (¾ hour from the road). The itinerary winds through the valley of the Golo river on the western side.

The head of the valley is dominated by the stark spectacle of the peaks of Capo Tafunata and Paglia Orba. Below, at the base of Col des Maures, you can see the distant Rifugio Ciottulu di I Mori (2,000 m/6,560 ft). To reach it the GR 20 bears left at the Bergeries de Tula (1,700 m/5,576 ft) and climbs sharply to the ridge on the western slope of the valley; then you head north in a semi-circle, among meadows and rocks, bringing this stage to a close.

Rifugio Ciottulu di I Mori to Rifugio di Tighjettu   H

7 km (4¼ miles), 3½ hours, change in elevation 230 m (754 ft) uphill, 600 m (1,968 ft) downhill

This is a preparatory stage for the next more strenuous stage of the GR 20; the route runs beneath the walls of Paglia Orba and Col de Foggiale (1,962 m/6,435 ft) and descends eastward along the steep slope of Foce Ghiallu valley. After passing through a forest of pines partly destroyed by old fires, you regain height, completing the circuit of the eastern buttresses of Paglia Orba. Crossing a ridge which barely divides the two valleys of Foce Ghiallu and the Viru river, you follow the course of the latter upward to the abandoned summer pasture of Ballone (1,440 m/4,723 ft; 2¾ hours) which has been turned into a refreshment spot. The demolished perimeter walls form a boundary to a sheltered space suitable for camping.

From Ballone there is a short walk up to Rifugio di Tighjettu. This recently opened building (1,640 m/5,379 ft) is ugly but spacious, replacing Rifugio Altore on the north side of Col Perdu, destroyed in 1985 by a fire and completely abandoned.

Rifugio di Tighjettu to Rifugio di Carrozzu   E

14.5 km (9 miles), 9 hours, change in elevation 1,020 m (3,345 ft) uphill, 1,480 m (4,854 ft) downhill

Here too it is best to press on to the distant Rifugio di

On pages 184 and 185: from Rifugio d'Asinao you can climb to the top of Mt Incudine, highest peak of the southern part of the itinerary.

The dark outline of a Corsican pine against the background of granitic walls: these trees, symbol of Corsica, still cover vast inland areas of the island.

Carrozzu, remaining up on the ridge rather than coming down to the hotel-restaurant of the Haut-Asco ski resort (5½ hours from Tighjettu) which has become the traditional stop since the destruction of the Rifugio Altore.

This is the most difficult stage of the entire GR 20, culminating in the crossing of the famous Cirque de la Solitude. Early in the morning, when the track is fortunately still shaded, you embark on the tiring climb northward across stony and rocky terrain up to Bocca Minuta (2,218 m/7,275 ft; 2 hours), on the brim of the Cirque de la Solitude, in a wild, stark landscape of rock walls and peaks. The descent is steep and strewn with boulders (be careful of falling stones dislodged by people above you) but presents no real difficulties even though there are exposed stretches with fixed ropes. The route encompasses a rock spur and then, again protected by ropes, leads up through a steep gorge and eventually reaches the pass of Col Perdu (2,184 m/7,163 ft; 1½ hours). The descent among boulders and snowfields, which vanish with the first heat, takes you past the small lakes at the base of the col to the ruins of Rifugio Altore.

A little lower down, the path branches right for Haut-Asco, once a detour but now marked with the standard red and white GR 20 sign. However, you keep to the old route which stays up high; after rounding the head of the Asco valley, there is a tiring ascent through a gorge to Bocca di Missodio, and finally a trek, with continuous ups and downs, along the line of the ridge beneath Punta Muvrella. The track now follows the western slope of the Muvrella and quickly loses height to reach Lake Muvrella (1,860 m/6,100 ft; 3½ hours), surrounded by thickets of alders. After a series of fairly easy climbs (fixed ropes), the GR 20 continues along the left side of the Spasimata valley, in a magnificent granite landscape. A suspended walkway takes you across the stream and on the opposite side you climb through the wood to Rifugio di Carrozzu (1,260 m/4,133 ft).

Detour – Excursion to the summit of Mt Cinto: from the Haut-Asco ski resort you can reach the highest point in Corsica (2,710 m/8,890 ft) after a five-hour walk.

Rifugio de Carrozzu to Rifugio de l'Ortu di u Piobbu   H

8 km (5 miles), 5 hours, change in elevation 950 m (3,116 ft) uphill, 660 m (2,165 ft) downhill

This is actually the new itinerary of the GR 20 which takes you along the ridge, in two stages, to Calenzana, after a serious fire half destroyed the forest of Bonifato, one of the loveliest in Corsica. The path behind the refuge climbs the valley in an eastward direction. Near the head of the valley, by now quite high, it bears north (left) and leads up through an area of sparse trees and boulders to Col de l'Inominata. The GR 20 leaves Punta di Ghialla on its right and continues an undulating course along the ridge, making a wide, high semi-circle beyond Col d'Avartoli (1,898 m/6,225 ft; 2½ hours) which leads to the pass (2,000 m/6,560 ft) between Punta Pischagia and Capu Ladroncellu.

There is a rock-strewn descent to the abandoned summer pasture of La Mandriaccia beyond the stream, and then another climb to the hilltop of Capu Giannone. From here a gentle descent along the hillside brings you to Rifugio Ortu di u Piobbu (1,570 m/5,150 ft), recently built beside the old *bergerie*.

Rifugio de l'Ortu di u Piobbia to Calenzana   H

11 km (6¾ miles), 5 hours, change in elevation 150 m (492 ft) uphill, 1,290 m (4,231 ft) downhill

Proceed around the head of the Malaghia valley and follow the slight gradient of the bend at the 1,500 m (4,920 ft) mark up to the ridge overlooking the Santucce summer pasture. The track points north, descending through meadows, and then west through the wood and over easy rock terrain. From the Col di Bocca u Saltu (1,250 m/4,100 ft; 2¼ hours), there is a twisting descent along the other side to the plain. After the descent, you continue on the level along a path bordered by barbed wire, as the rugged scenery of ridges gives way to Mediterranean maquis with the chirp of crickets. A final spurt takes you up to the small ridge leading away from the junction with the "Mountain and Sea Road." At a point where you can look over the plain towards the sea, there is a mule track to Calenzana (275 m/902 ft). From here a local bus service runs to the coastal town of Calvi, bringing the trip to an end.

DURMITOR PARK

Over the pasturelands of Montenegro

The Durmitor National Park, opened in 1978, covers part of the Montenegrin plateau, which is situated between the Sušica and Tara rivers and the Tara canyon, in an area bounded by the confluences of the Tara with the Bistrica to the south and the Sušica to the north.

In a comparatively restricted region, karstic geological features together with the erosive effects of the last Ice Age have combined to create an area of particularly uneven, rugged terrain which, because of its variety and beauty, is ideal for walking and climbing.

Flora and fauna

From the village of Ivan Do, only a few minutes from the famous Black Lake (Crno Jezero) at the foot of the Medjed, bridle paths lead up to the summer pastures among forests of fir and spruce, passing first through woods of conifer, and, above the 1,600 m (5,250 ft) mark, of beech, the last remains of immense forests which once covered the whole territory. Beyond the beech wood is the karstic upland plain, pastureland for flocks and herds during the summer transhumance. Here, dark green mugo pines (locally called *klerk*) cluster on the slopes, sometimes gentle, sometimes steep, of the characteristic funnel-shaped depressions known as dolines.

In these high meadows a myriad of small and delicate mountain flowers – soldanellas, violas,

Useful addresses: Uprava Nac. Parka "Durmitora" (Park Management), 84220 Žabljak, Yugoslavia.
Map: "Durmitor and Tara Canyon" (Durmitor National Park) – 1:25,000 "Mountain Map," obtainable with guide from the park offices.
Bibliography: *Durmitor and the Tara Canyon*, Durmitor National Park, Žabljak, Geokarta Cartography Bureau, Belgrade.

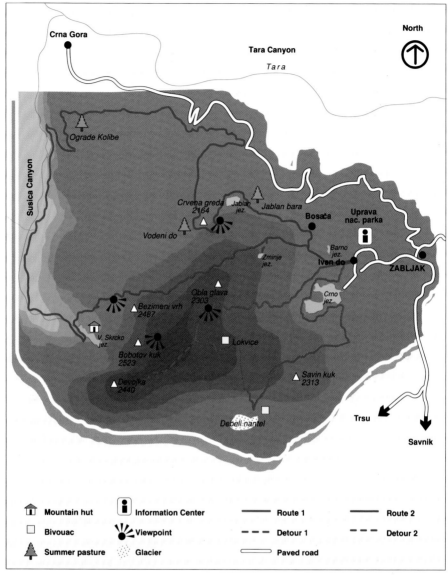

Distance: Two round trips of two and three days, 19 and 39 km (11¾ and 24 miles) respectively, which cover the range of natural surroundings in the park.

Departure and arrival points: The village of Ivan Do (1,468 m/4,815 ft), 2 km from the tourist resort of Žabljak; regular coach service links Žabljak to the coast (Dubrovnik via Nikšić) or the hinterland (Belgrade via Pljevla and Titograd via Nikšić). Flights and ferry services from Dubrovnik.

Where to stay: Hotels at Žabljak or, better still, bed and breakfast accommodation at Ivan Do; mountain huts along the route; tents are indispensable for other overnight stops, detours and unplanned stops.

Signposting: White discs encircled in red and red markings virtually everywhere on the route. At important junctions there are directional signs.

Difficulty: E – expert hikers.

When to go: End June, July, August, September; in early summer some stretches are still snowbound and inadvisable except with suitable equipment.

Equipment: Apart from the usual accessories for mid- and high-mountain treks, sufficient food must be taken to cover the journey, although this can be supplemented with local produce bought from shepherds.

gentians and anemones – create a riot of colour in the summer.

Deep in the Durmitor canyon, in an atmosphere where the humidity factor is markedly increased, the lush vegetation consists of a mixed woodland of broadleaved species while, among the conifers growing high along the rim, there are occasional sturdy specimens of mountain pine, rooted in the most inaccessible crags.

The wild animals of the region, rare and seldom encountered, shrink from the presence of humans who for centuries have hunted in these valleys. Small groups of chamois inhabit the highest and remotest zones; many foxes roam the pastures and forests, squirrels scamper through the trees, but traces of bears and wolves, though recognizable, are less frequent. Birds, however, present in greater numbers, include the black woodpecker and the hazel hen, which live in the conifer belt around Crno Jezero, and, among raptors, the golden eagle and peregrine.

The people of Durmitor

Nature is not the only attraction of the Durmitor region. The people, too, are an interesting feature, and it is very rewarding to find out about how the local shepherds lead their lives. They spend the winter in the valley in the characteristic houses with high-pitched roofs, surrounded by a couple of feet of snow. Then from June to September all those not involved with the small tourist industry leave Žabljak and Mala Crna Gora to take their herds up to the pastures. Those still used are Ograde Kolibe, a complete summer village in miniature, and a number of others scattered along the mouths of valleys, such as Katun Lokvice. In the morning, after milking, the boys take the cattle out to pasture and only return at dusk, travelling perhaps more than 10 km (6 miles). The adults stay behind to look after the huts and handle the milk, making cheese to sell and yoghurt for family consumption. So during the day there are mainly elderly folk around the village who, no longer at work, spend their time chatting and remembering the past, especially their partisan activities in the Second World War.

Life in the mountains is simple and still very primitive: long journeys are still made on horseback and in

OVERNIGHT STAYS

At Žabljak overnight tourist accommodation is relatively easy to find either in hotels or in bed and breakfast accommodation.

At Ivan Do, the small village which is the departure point for the suggested itineraries not far from Crno Jezero, there is a field reserved for camping but the best solution, as it is in Žabljak, is to look for private accommodation, easily found by chatting with the locals.

On the first round trip, you can choose to stay overnight in either of two mountain huts: the first, at Velika Kalica (2,020 m/6,625 ft), is a barrel-shaped structure in wood and metal sheeting (6/10 persons) close to the glacier at the head of the glacial cirque (stove and cooking utensils, supply of melted snow water); the second, at Lokvice, has ten beds on planking (two huts, wood stove only) with a spring not far away.

On the second round trip, you may need a tent because overnight stays are possible only in the mountain hut managed by forest rangers of Lake Škrčko (1,723 m/5,651 ft) with bunk beds for 25 people and bedrooms for 4 people. Open from mid June to end September, it offers the use of a kitchen and a wood stove, with drinking water and toilets outside. The charge is modest and you should carry all the food you need. A hotel-refuge (known as a motel) is in the process of being opened on the Šusičko Jezero.

It is also possible, however, to camp near mountain huts mentioned above, using their facilities, and at various other places along the route marked on the guide book.

On page 190 and 191: from the Medjedje Zdrijelo saddle there is a panoramic view over the meadows of the Alisnica glacial depression which still have patches of snow in early summer.

the evening huts are lit by candlelight or oil lamp. Bread is baked at home in wood ovens and the diet is very sparse: milk, yoghurt, cheese, with neither fruit nor vegetables. In the more isolated summer pastures, the floor of the huts consists of bare earth and the shepherds spend the night together on huge wooden beds.

The itinerary

The map shows a huge network of paths, traditionally used for summer transhumance, and nowadays mostly marked. So for anyone planning a trip to the mountains of Durmitor there is a wide choice of routes.

The ideal solution is to plan circular routes which bring you back to your point of departure. From the village of Ivan Do, therefore, we suggest two round trips. The first is shorter, through meadow and mountain scenery, and although requiring only one overnight stop, introduces you to the wild, rugged environment of the highest peaks. The second, more varied, gives you a sample of the diverse habitats of the park, taking you through the outlying zones of tableland and karstic dolines, meadows and summer pastures, and the varied landscapes of forests, canyons and lakes.

The two proposed routes can be partially linked to form a single itinerary lasting several days which combine the principal features of both; should you do this, however, it is advisable, before setting off, to check on conditions on several passes that may still be snowbound in late summer and would thus be difficult (if not impossible) to negotiate without suitable equipment.

First round trip

Ivan Do to Velika Kalica mountain hut   E

9 km (6 miles), 4 hours, change in elevation 600 m (1,968 ft) uphill, 50 m (165 ft) downhill

From Ivan Do (1,468 m/4,815 ft) you will easily find the unmarked path that descends through the forest to Crno Jezero (Black Lake), the clear water of which reflects the grandiose Medjed massif (2,170 m/7,117 ft). The lake is formed by two basins, the Veliko (Large) Jezero and the Malo (Small) Jezero,

THE TARA CANYON

For those with more time at their disposal, the River Tara canyon offers magnificent scenery and the opportunity of alternative treks to those of the Durmitor mountain environment. Here the chemical and mechanical eroding action of the Tara has cut a gorge, 84 km (52 miles) long and 1,600 m (5,250 ft) deep, into the karstic terrain. The river flows in a series of deep, calm pools, surrounded by waterfalls and dense woodland, widening in some parts to form broad valleys. Here, shepherds have set up their huts, making every possible use of the available pasture land (photograph below). The bed of the canyon is negotiable by canoe or kayak over its first stretch only, from Bistrica to Šljivansko (21 km/13 miles). From Šljivansko (Splavište) to Šćepan Polje where the Tara and Piva join to form the Drina, the course of the river is equally spectacular but calmer, and can be covered on log rafts or rubber dinghies. At the bottom of the canyon a mountain hut and area for tents have been set up for hikers. Rafting on the river is organized by Montenegroturist, with booking three months in advance, or by other groups, which need to be contacted only a few weeks beforehand. Information may be obtained from the guide Goan Leković, Durdevica Tara, 84223 Kosanica, or from the proprietor of the motel in Kosanica.

HISTORY OF MONTENEGRO

Probably impelled by the migrations of the Avari, the Slavs reached the Montenegro region in the seventh century and subjugated the Illyrian and Celtic people who lived there. With the conversion to orthodox Christianity in 870 and, a century later, with the invasion of the Magyar peoples who separated them from their brothers in the north, the Slavs of Serbia and Montenegro moved eastward, linking themselves to the Greek culture of Constantinople, and in the succeeding centuries to the orthodox land of Imperial Russia.

The invasion of the Balkan peninsula by the Turks in the fourteenth century was the crucial moment in the history of Montenegro: deprived of an outlet to the sea, the region was thrust into the front line of battle against the infidels. For more than 500 years the Montenegrins were engaged in wars against the Ottoman Empire, and, thanks to their courage and harsh territory, managed to preserve their independence.

The alliance with Imperial Russia, initiated in the eighteenth century by Peter the Great, constituted a turning point in the story of this continuing conflict. Alongside the Russians in the Napoleonic Wars and in successive campaigns against the Ottomans, the Montenegrins managed to conquer and win recognition to an outlet on the Adriatic in 1878, even though they had to wait until the Second Balkan War, in 1913, to be freed finally from the threat of Turkey.

Montenegro became part of the newly established Yugoslavia after the First World War but was again compelled to take up arms against the invader, in the Second World War. The epic of partisan resistance is still kept alive in the stories of old shepherds who remember with pride their courageous guerilla actions against the Germans and Italians. When peace finally came Montenegro emerged as one of the six socialist republics that nowadays form the Federation of Yugoslavia.

which, as a result of the natural drainage of water across the karstic bed, have become separated and are joined by a narrow strip of land.

From the lake follow the turning with direction signs for the peaks of Savin Kuk and Medjed, and bear right, making an almost complete circle of the two basins, along a wide path with benches for enjoying the views. At the crossroads take the mule track which branches away from the shore and climbs through the conifer wood. At Točak, turn right shortly after the spring, following the signs for Medjed and Velika Kalica. As you get higher, broadleaved trees replace the conifers and eventually thin out completely; and beyond the path branching off to the Medjed ridge you reach the wild landscape of the Velika Kalica glacial cirque, a vast ampitheater dominated by the third peak of Durmitor (Sljeme, 2,455 m/8,052 ft). Continue along the edge of the long valley dotted with snowfields (in June there are some steep stretches which must be negotiated with care) on the southern foothills of Veliki Medjed until you come, after a gentle climb, to the mountain hut (2,020 m/6,625 ft) set up not far from the front of the Debeli Namet glacier, the only one left in the region.

Velika Kalica mountain hut to Ivan Do   E

10 km (6¼ miles), 5¼ hours, change in elevation 485 m (1,590 ft) uphill, 1,035 m (3,395 ft) downhill

From the hut continue climbing towards Velika Previja across snowfields and rocky ground which is especially steep in places. There is a marvellous view from the pass over much of the central mountain area of Durmitor, a spectacular landscape of snow-covered cirques and mighty peaks.

You now descend by a path which is not always clearly marked, steeply at first and then diagonally along the Medjed foothills through the valley that leads to the Lokvice pastures. Adjacent to the mountain houses and pens, two small huts constitute somewhat spartan resting places for those who decide to prolong the first stage. The itinerary now proceeds westward along the path which, beyond the nearby spring, runs diagonally across the steep slopes of Čvorov Bogaz. The climb continues to bear right up the sides of the rock- and detritus-strewn valley, and after 40 minutes reaches an intersection: in one direction is an old track, no longer used, towards

Ledena Pécina, and in the other is the marked route to the summit of Minin Bogaz. This involves a further 50 minutes' strenuous climbing over rocks and snow-fields, still around in July, past the junction for Bobotov Kuk until, on the highest bends of the Biljegov Do, you reach the famous Cave of Ice, the Ledena Pécina. The physical effort is now rewarded, just before reaching the pass, with one of the most spectacular views of the Durmitor region: to south-south-east the peaks of Terzin Bogaz and Savin Kuk, to the south-south-west that of Bobotov Kuk and, in the distance, part of the route already done, from Velika Previja down through the glacial depression of Bavani. The Cave of Ice, concealed farther north below the Obla Glava massif, has its mysterious entrance at the end of a steep strip of perpetual snow. An ice axe, crampons, rope and a strong torch are useful accessories for exploring the cave and admiring the extraordinary ice sculptures on the walls.

From Ledena Pécina you descend rapidly and steeply across snowfields that are still there until late summer, and eventually rejoin the marked path

Above: the village of Ivan Do.
Below: while the men take the animals out to pasture, the old people and the children remain in the village.

which winds through a strange karstic landscape to the old summer pastures of Stari Katun. After crossing the junction with the path from the Lokvice hut you leave behind the bleak landscape of rock gorges and plunge into woodland along a mule track that leads down to the first houses of Ivan Do, where the round trip comes to an end.

Suggested detour

On the second stage, the ascent of Bobotov Kuk, the highest peak (2,523 m/8,275 ft), with a 360° view of the entire Durmitor group and its deep canyons, is recommended for experts with suitable equipment, until late summer. You should reckon on at least 4 hours there and back from the junction on the route to Biljegov Do. The mountain hut marked on the map at Valvoviti Do has been destroyed.

Above: a summer pasture.
Below: Jablua Jezero, one of the Durmitor National Park's glacial lakes.

Second round trip

Ivan Do to Škrčko Jezero mountain hut H

11.5 (7 miles), 5½ hours, change in elevation 900 m (2,952 ft) uphill, 645 m (2,115 ft) downhill

Just past the last houses of Ivan Do (1,468 m/4,815 ft) take the right branch off the dirt road and climb into the wood. Passing Lake Barno, situated in a boggy depression surrounded by conifers, the marked path joins a dirt road which soon comes to the junction for Zminje Jezero; it is worth extending the trip slightly to visit this lake, tucked like a jewel in the silence of the wood; and you can stock up with water from the spring on its western shore. Among age-old trees, the last specimens of an ancient forest, the dirt track becomes a bridle path and then, as the climb gets more difficult, tapers away as it approaches the pastures of Crepuljna Poljana (1,700 m/5,576 ft). From here, over increasingly open ground, the path follows a twisting course along a moraine which leads to the glacial zone ofAlišnica (1,950 m/6,396 ft) and continues through lush, undulating meadows still flecked with snow and fed by small pools in which the animals slake their thirst. High above, the limestone rocks have assumed bizarre forms, corroded and carved into strange shapes by karstick activity. Over the saddle of Medjedje Ždrijelo (2,251 m/7,383 ft) you soon reach the verdant plain of Planinica (2,330 m/7,642 ft), which provides a magnificent panorama of the Bezimeni Vrh, Bobotov Kuk and Djevojka massifs to the south-east and an incomparable bird's-eye view of the Malo and Veliko Škrčko lakes below, with a glimpse between them of the hut which is the destination of this stage (1,723 m/5,651 ft).

Škrčko Jezero hut to Ograde Kolibe H

11 km (6¾ miles), about 4½ hours, change in elevation 425 m (1,394 ft) uphill, 550 m (1,804 ft) downhill

From the hut you retrace part of the previous day's route, walking down to the lake shore where a marked path forks off to the left. Today's stage reveals a new aspect of the Durmitor region: after a steep, twisting descent alongside the beautiful Skakala waterfall, you enter the narrow valley of the Sušica river, through canyon landscape that truly

BIOGRADSKA GORA NATIONAL PARK

Features: Not far from the Durmitor, the Biogradska Gora National Park has an area almost wholly covered by one of the last virgin forests in Europe; Montenegro beech, ash, silver fir, sycamore and mountain pine form a vast woodland zone which blankets the steep hillsides.

Access and information center: The park is close to the Belgrade–Bar railway line, just 93 km (58 miles) from Titograd. Access to the park is on the road to Mojkovac. On the shore of Lake Biogradsko is an area set up as a camping site, the house of the forest rangers and a small sloping-roofed restaurant. Information available on the spot, or apply to the Turistički Savez Crne Gore, Bulvar Lenjina 2/1, Titograd.

Trekking in the park: Close to the camping site there are several marked paths which soon take you up through huge meadows to viewpoints high over the Biogradska forest. It is also interesting to take the path which, likewise leaving from the camping site area, follows the right bank of the lake and then, inside the forest, climbs the Biogradska river to its source.

At sunset the village of Ograde Kolibe comes to life with the return of the shepherds and their flocks; but very soon all is silent as the sheep of each owner are shut up in their pens.

reflects the Durmitor region in its wildest guise. The track, sometimes very muddy, winds through tangled vegetation which grows freely in this particularly humid natural environment. When you see the bed of the stream, you can observe how the flow of water sinks at intervals into the ground, vanishing and reappearing at points in the undergrowth. This proof of karstic phenomenon is again evident on arrival at the broad clearing of the Sušičko Jezero, occupied, depending on the season, by the lake or by a spongy carpet of grass and moss. On the north bank a hotel-refuge has recently been opened.

You now leave the valley and climb the cutting up to the edge of the plateau, from where you can see the deep furrow etched out by the Sušica, and branch off right to the village of Ograde Kolibe (1,595 m/5,231 ft), summer transhumance home for the inhabitants of the village of Mala Crna Gora, and the destination of this second stage. By offering a small sum of money, you will get permission to pitch a tent close to the shepherds' huts and to enjoy their hospitality and an atmosphere which becomes even livelier at sunset when the herds return from pasture.

Ograde Kolibe to Ivan Do H

16 km (10 miles), about 7½ hours, change in elevation 610 m (2,000 ft) uphill, 730 m (2,394 ft) downhill

Heading east from the village, you cross a landscape in which dolines alternate with undulating green slopes, the tops of which appear to be sprinkled with snow but which are actually covered by a white hood of limestone. The track, at first self-evident and later marked in red, leads you south-eastward up through the wood, to the left of the dirt road and its hairpin bends which run from the village of Mala Crna Gora to Žabljak. On the horizon, to the north-east, the plateau suddenly sinks to form the Tara canyon.

The path, not always well marked, ascends through mugo pines and then comes down to a bend in the road where the route to the summit of Crvena Greda branches off to the west. The track continues up and down along the hillside, around the southern slopes of the Pazišta, and then makes a broad semi-circle to reach the Gologlav hill and the abandoned summer pastures of Vodeni Do, formerly among the highest in Montenegro. The route runs through the famous "Klek Labyrinth" (of mugo pines), a tangled maze whose secret paths, now marked, were once known only to shepherds. The climb up to the rock mass of Crvena Greda provides you with a last look at the Durmitor landscape before you begin the long descent to Ivan Do which ends the itinerary. Still up hill, you encircle the basin of the Jablan Jezero, hemmed in between the projecting walls of the Crvena Greda and Mala Greda; then you come down, past old mountain houses, to the idyllic pastures of Jablan Bara (water fountain). Continuing down through the meadows, you eventually see the basin of the Crno Jezero, surrounded by conifers, and, tucked away in the distance among the pines, the houses of Ivan Do. Past the spur of Razana Glava you enter into the wood and below the village of Bosača (water fountain) you are back at the first stage of the itinerary.

At the foot of the Mala Greda, the meadows around the houses of the now abandoned pasture of Jablan Bara can be used for camping.

MOUNT ATHOS TOUR

Tracing the monasteries of the Halkidiki peninsula

Mount Athos is the most easterly of the three promontories of the peninsula of Halkidiki which jut out like a trident into the Aegean Sea, in northern Greece. The Athonite promontory is about 45 km (30 miles) long and some 5–10 km (3–6 miles) wide, and it is joined to the mainland by an isthmus only 2 km (1¼ miles) across. The promontory is bisected by a mountainous spine which rises progressively from the 510 m (1,672 ft) of the Megali Vigla (meaning Great Look-out) to the 1,042 m (3,417 ft) of the so-called Antithonas. And at the southern tip of the peninsula, rising sheer over the Aegean, is the rocky, pyramid-shaped mass of Mount Athos (2,033 m/6,668 ft).

The sea is calm and clear along the coasts, especially the south-western shore, but at the most southerly point it is dangerous because of the double confluence of ocean currents and winds. The coastlines consist, what is more, of high, jagged cliffs, although they are punctuated by numerous inlets.

The hills are covered by dense Mediterranean maquis, made up of laurels, myrtles, wild roses and junipers interspersed with cypresses, olives and Judas trees. Above 500 m (1,640 ft) this gives way to woods of oak, plane, lime, beech, chestnut, fir and pine. Around the monasteries and other monastic houses, fruit trees grow in abundance, while the exceptional fertility of the soil (once described in a legend as the Garden of the Virgin) permits the cultivation of all kinds of vegetables.

Useful addresses: National Tourism Organization (EOT), 8, Aristotelous Square, Thessaloniki, Greece. Tel.: (0)31/271888.
Hellenic Alpine Club, Karalou D:1 15, Thessaloniki. Tel.: (0)31/278888.
Map: The most reliable map is the Austrian one published by Reinhold Zwerger, 1:50,000 (Wohlmutstrasse 8, A 1020 Vienna).
Bibliography: T. Salmon, *The Mountains of Greece*, Cicerone Press, Cumbria.

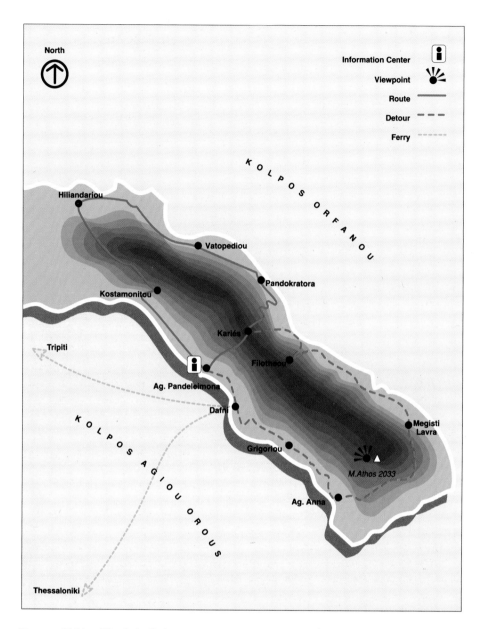

Distance: 46.5 km (29 miles), divided into four stages.

Departure point: Kariés, capital of the monastic republic. Access: from Thessaloniki by bus to Ouranopoli (134 km/83 miles; 3 hours; hotels and pensions for overnight stay). From Ouranopoli transfer by ferry to Athos harbour of Dafni (daily service with departures at 10 a.m.; in summer twice daily with departures early morning and midday; length of voyage 1¾ hours); from Dafni transfer by bus to Kariés (connecting with ferry service; length of journey 30 minutes).

Arrival point: Landing stage of Kostamonitou monastery on west coast; boat to Ouranopoli.

Where to stay: Along the route, overnight stays at the monasteries of Pandokratora, Vatopediou, Hiliandariou and Kostamonitou.

Signposting: Signposts indicate the direction to the various monasteries and their annexes.

Difficulty: R – ramblers, easy.

When to go: Spring (April to June) and autumn (September-October).

Equipment: Low altitude.

Monastic life

The origin of monasticism on Mount Athos (or, to be precise, the Holy Mountain, in Greek *Aghíon Oros*) is attributed to Ossios Athanassios (St Athanasius) who in 963 founded the first monastery there, the Megisti Lavra, and organized it according to the rule of St Basil. The imperial ratification or *typikon*, granted in 972, still represents the basic charter which regulates today's theocratic republic and which prohibits entry, among others, to women, eunuchs and minors.

The reason why monasteries came to be established here is to be sought in the natural characteristics of the region and in the political events of the eighth and ninth centuries. On the one hand, the isolation and inaccessibility of the peninsula made such places ideal for the contemplative life; on the other, expansion of Arab power and the collapse of monastic centers in Egypt, Syria and Asia Minor, as well as the hostility of the Byzantine emperors to monastic life during the iconoclastic period, resulted in an influx of monks from every part of the Empire.

The Mount Athos community always preserved its independence even under Turkish rule and this special privilege was confirmed successively by the Greek kingdom and republic. Today some 1,500 monks live on the Athonite promontory, as against the 8,000 at the time of its greatest splendour, divided among 20 monasteries which look from the outside like fortified citadels, complete with battlements and watch towers. Inside, their masterpieces constitute a rich museum of Byzantine culture.

The various monasteries are connected by a series of paved paths or tracks which are only negotiable on foot and are well signposted throughout. The meticulous paving work dates back to the middle of the seventeenth century and was carried out on the instructions of the patriarch of Constantinople. But there is a road linking the small harbour of Dafni with the capital, Kariés, and from here to the Iviron monastery. Every day the ferry from Ouranopoli arrives in Dafni with monks and pilgrims who take the bus to the capital.

Trekking on Mount Athos, for those permitted to enter, provides the chance to spend a few days in the sheer natural beauty of the Mediterranean landscape and to see the different aspects of monastic life.

ENTRY FORMALITIES

Entry to Mount Athos is confined to male individuals aged over 15 years who express a specific interest in the Holy Monastic area. Minors have to be accompanied by their father or someone taking responsibility for them. Permission is restricted to a maximum of ten visitors a day, except for those of Greek nationality. Formalities entail the issuing of a series of permission certificates:
1. A letter of recommendation from your country's embassy or consulate. (e.g. British Consulate, 8 Venizelou Str., Eleftherias Square. Tel.: (0)31/278006). The permit must be requested in writing and include personal details, reason for visit and date required. The consulate books entry to Mount Athos with the Ministry of Northern Greece at Thessaloniki. The introductory letter must be collected at least one day before the proposed visit.
2. Authorization of entry to Mount Athos granted by the Ministry of Northern Greece in Thessaloniki or the Ministry of Foreign Affairs in Athens on presentation of introductory letter. Ministry of Northern Greece, Dioikitiriou Square, 1st floor, Room 218, tel. (0)31/270092; open to public Monday to Friday 10 a.m. to 2 p.m.
3. The *diamonitírion* issued by the Holy Epistasia in Kariés. The permit is obtainable from the Palace of the Holy Community at Kariés on presentation of passport and authorization of the Ministry of Northern Greece. The *diamonitírion* is normally valid for a maximum of four days.

Behaviour and dress are expected to be in keeping with the holiness of the area. Photographs are allowed but not cine cameras.

THE SOUTHERN TRAIL

The southern circuit links all the principal monasteries situated at the tip of the Athonite promontory.

It covers a distance of 60 km (37 miles) and can be done in five stages:

1st stage: Kariés – Koutloumoussiou – Iviron – Filotheou (9.5 km/6 miles; 2¾ hours).

2nd stage: Filotheou – Karakalou – Megisti Lavra (18 km/11 miles; 5¾ hours).

3rd stage: Megisti Lavra – Agia Anna (14 km/8¾ miles; 3¾ hours).

4th stage: Agia Anna – Agiu Pavlou – Dionissiou – Ossiou Grigoriou (9 km/5 ½ miles; 3¾ hours).

5th stage: Ossiou Grigoriou – Simona Petras – Dafni (9.5 km/6 miles; 3 hours).

The southern circuit, together with the northern circuit described in the main text, makes an itinerary of 11 stages which takes you right around the Athonite promontory.

The itinerary

Because of monastic regulations, this trek is restricted to male visitors. Women are permitted to go as far as Ouranopoli.

The suggested itinerary is broken down into three stages which link the monasteries in the northern sector of the Athos promontory. For the most part, the trek is on old paved paths that run through Mediterranean scrubland, from sea level to altitudes of about 500 m (1,640 ft). So there are no great changes of elevation and, as a rule, just a succession of easy ups and downs.

The stages are planned so as to allow you to reach the monastery where you will be spending the night early in the afternoon, thus giving you time to visit the buildings, participate in the religious services and, should it be a coenobitic establishment (where there is a communal way of life), to share a meal with the monks.

If you can get an extended permit, you may complete the northern circuit by spending the night at Agiu Pandeleimona and then going on to Dafni.

Kariés to Pandokratora   R

8 km (5 miles), 2½ hours, change in elevation 450 m (1,476 ft) uphill, 100 m (320 ft) downhill

The first part of the day is spent transferring by boat from Ouranopoli to Dafni and then travelling by bus to Kariés (350 m/1,148 ft). After obtaining your permit, the *diamonitírion*, from the Palace of the Holy Community, before setting out on the walk it is worth visiting the church of the Protatos at Kariés, which is the oldest building on Mount Athos (mid tenth century).

A dirt road winds down along the eastern side of the peninsula towards the Iviron monastery. After about 3 km (1¾ miles) a junction to the left indicates the way to the Stavronikita monastery which soon appears on the seacoast, looking like a medieval castle with powerful crenellated walls and towers. It accommodates 16 young monks, most of them Greek (5.5 km/3½ miles; 1½ hours). From Stavronikita a twisting path runs north along the hill through the maquis, leading to the monastery of Pandokratora, perched on a rock promontory overlooking a picturesque bay (2.5 km/1½ miles; 1 hour). Here live 15 or

On pages 204 and 205: the Greek coenobitic monastery of Simona Petras. Founded in the fourteenth century, it stands on the southwestern coast.

Opposite: the Serbian monastery of Hiliandariou.

so elderly Greek monks, according to the idiorrhythmic rule (living individually and only coming together to pray). Features of interest here are the *katholikón*, the walls of which are decorated with frescoes of the Macedonian school (fourteenth century), and the refectory with its eighteenth-century frescoes.

Pandokratora to Vatopediou R

9 km (5½ miles), 2¾ hours, change in elevation 350 m (1,148 ft) uphill, 400 m (1,312 ft) downhill

The path to Vatopediou continues through the hills behind the Pandokratora monastery, emerging at the top of a hill some 400 m (1,312 ft) above sea level and then coming down to the broad bay of Vatopediou. The path up which you climb is the old one that was paved in the mid seventeenth century; then it joins a new dirt road linking the capital to the Vatopediou monastery, which constitutes an alternative, quicker but less attractive, route to the track.

The bell tower and katholikón *(church) of the Greek monastery of Vatopediou, second most important of the Mount Athos monasteries.*

A detour off the main route will take you to the Russian *skíti* (a rural cell where monks live away from the monastery in recluse) of Prophet Elias and Bogoroditsa, both occupied by young monks of Russian origin.

The Vatopediou monastery, following the idiorrhythmic rule and accommodating 15 monks, ranks second in importance after the Megisti Lavra. It is the only one to have adopted the Gregorian calendar. The most interesting buildings are the *katholikón*, the very graceful *fiáli*, a small circular construction for blessing water, and the eighteenth-century refectory with marble tables dating from the twelfth century.

Vatopediou to Hiliandariou   R

14 km (8¾ miles), 4 hours, change in elevation 300 m (984 ft) uphill, 250 m (820 ft) downhill

The walk from Vatopediou to Hiliandariou is the most enjoyable part of the trek since it runs entirely through the lush and highly scented wilderness of Mediterranean maquis. After several gentle rises and descents, you reach a height of almost 200 m (650 ft) and then come down to the first stopping point of the day, the monastery of Esfigmenou, situated at the end of a small bay (10.5 km/6½ miles; 3 hours). From here it is only 3.5 km (2 miles) to Hiliandariou (1 hour) and it is worth taking a detour to the bay where the St Basil Tower, locally known as Hrusija, stands.

The tower fortress, built on a rock promontory, dates back to the early fourteenth century and was constructed by the Serbian king Milutin to defend the area. The creeks to the north of the tower, with their beaches of very fine sand, offer the chance of a well-earned rest before resuming the walk to Hiliandariou. This monastery is situated in a delightful valley full of dense vegetation and is the home of some 20 monks. The perimeter monastic buildings surround a huge courtyard at the bottom of which is the fourteenth-century *katholikón* and in front of it a charming *fiáli*. The Hiliandariou *katholikón*, with its elegant two- and three-light windows, decorated with marble and ornamental bas-reliefs, and its graceful cupolas, is the loveliest example of Byzantine architecture on Mount Athos.

The monastery's kitchen serves the best meals and most delicious wine in the Athos region.

GLOSSARY

Anaghnóstis = monk employed to read in the refectory.

Apódipnon = celebration of evening liturgy.

Archontaríki = monastery guest room.

Archontáris = monk employed to arrange meals and accommodation for visitors.

Arsanáris = monk employed at landing stage of monastery.

Arsanás = landing stage.

Dochíon = general food store.

Dochiáris = monk employed as storekeeper.

Epitropía = monastic organ of government and administration.

Esperinós = celebration of afternoon liturgy.

Fiáli = small circular-plan building with a cupola; in the center is a fountain of holy water.

Icona = sacred painting done on a portable panel.

Igumeneo = superior of a coenobitic monastery.

Katholikón = principal church of the Byzantine monasteries.

Kélle = monastic cells.

Mághiras = monk employed as cook.

Maghirion = kitchen.

Portáris = monk employed to receive visitors.

Proestós = superior of an idiorrhythmic monastery.

Vivliotíki = library.

MONASTIC ORGANIZATION

Although subject to the sovereignty of Greece, Mount Athos enjoys a privileged system of government recognized and guaranteed by the Greek constitution. The Holy Community is its central authority, this being composed of representatives from the monasteries which, united in a permanent body, exercise administrative and judicial powers. Executive power, however, is vested in the Holy Epistasia (Superintendence), a committee of four monks, one of whom is appointed Protepistate (President) of the Athonite republic.

There are 20 monasteries (17 Greek, one Russian, one Serbian and one Bulgarian) and a number of other communities dependent on them: *skíti*, smaller monastic foundations; *kellía*, agricultural communities; *kalíve*, small buildings where tiny groups of monks lead austere lives; *kathísmata*, individual buildings near monasteries; and *issichastíria*, secluded hermitages.

The monasteries are divided into two categories, according to two different rules of life: coenobitic and idiorrhythmic. In coenobitic monasteries all activities (work, prayer and meals) are carried out communally under the direction of a superior, the *igumeneo*; in idiorrhythmic monasteries only prayer is communal while work and meals are left to the monks' individual initiative.

Meals are very frugal and mainly vegetarian, based on bread, olives, tomatoes, potatoes, lentils and other vegetables.

On Mount Athos the Julian calendar is still in force, so that in order to determine the date there 13 days have to be subtracted from the Gregorian calendar. The hours of the day are calculated according to Byzantine time where zero hour falls at sunset.

Most of today's 1,500 resident monks are of Greek nationality but there are also Russians, Serbs, Bulgarians and Romanians, as well as representatives of Western countries.

Hiliandariou to Kostamonitou   R

12.5 km (7¾ miles), 4 hours, change in elevation 450 m (1,476 ft) uphill, 300 m (984 ft) downhill

The path from the monastery of Hiliandariou to the monastery of Zografou and thence to that of Kostamonitou runs down the Athos promontory from north to south, linking its north-eastern and south-western slopes.

Beyond Hiliandariou the path makes an abrupt climb through dense bushland to a height of about 300 m (984 ft) above sea level. From here to the imposing Bulgarian monastery of Zografou the walk is all gently downhill along a mostly paved track (8.5 km/5¼ miles; 2¼ hours).

From Zografou to Kostamonitou, however, the path leads continuously up and down and although, as the crow flies, the two monasteries are fairly close, the walk takes longer than might be expected (4 km/2½ miles; 1¾ hours). The Greek monastery of Kostamonitou is built on the southern slope of a picturesque valley. It follows the coenobite rule and is inhabited by about 20 monks, most of them Greek,

and is the last in the monastic hierarchy. After an overnight stay at Kostamonitou, you can head for its landing stage the following morning (½ hour), and from here you take the boat to the Greek village of Ouranopoli.

Detour: If you can get your visiting permit extended, you can complete the northern circuit of Mount Athos in two stages, ending the trip at Dafni.

Kostamonitou – Dohiariou – Xenofonda – Agiu Pandeleimona 10 km (6¼ miles); 3¼ hours; the walk from Xenofonda begins on the road south of the monastery. After about 500 m, at the end of the climb just before the left bend, you leave the road and continue along the path which bears right.

Agiu Pandeleimona – Xiropotamou – Dafni 5 km (3 miles); 1½ hours; the path from Agiu Pandeleimona to the port of Xiropotamou is not in use but it is easy to keep sight of it from the seashore. The path which descends from Xiropotamou to its landing stage meets the Dafni-Kariés road at the modern bridge behind the landing stage itself. From here continue along the road.

Above: Father Stefan, anchorite (a hermit) of the Greek skíti *of Kofsokali, situated at the southern tip of the Athonite promontory.*

Below: the picturesque arsanás *(landing stage) of the Bulgarian monastery of Sografu.*

INDEX